DORLING KINDERSLEY  EYEWITNESS BOOKS

FORCE &
MOTION

Late 19th-century carpenter's plane

Bronze-Age axe head

Universal joint, 1935

BUDDING

Gyroscopic globe

Model of Greek water mill

18th-century apparatus demonstrating the lifting power of the pulley

Toothed gear-wheel
from a calendar
clock c. AD 500

DK EYEWITNESS BOOKS

FORCE & MOTION

Written by
PETER LAFFERTY

A spinning
gyroscope

Screw
threads

Twin-cylinder
aircraft engine

The first
lawn-mower c.1830

A pendulum clock
designed by Galileo
Galilei, built in 1883

Dorling Kindersley

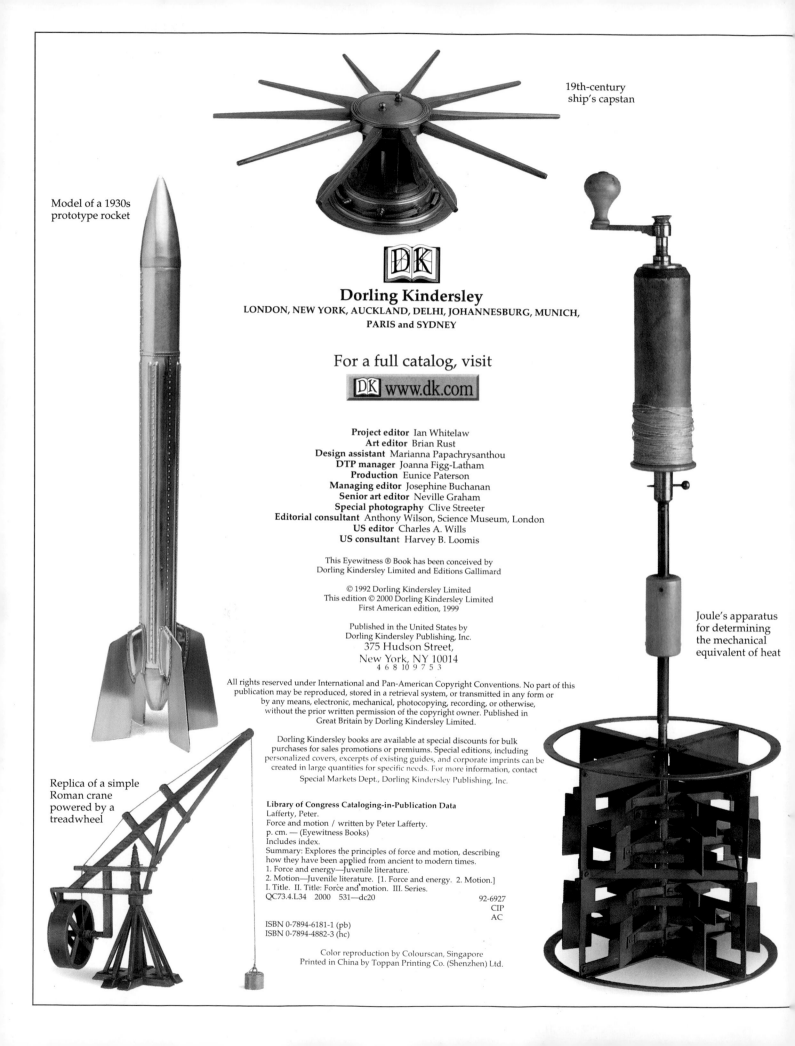

Model of a 1930s
prototype rocket

19th-century
ship's capstan

Dorling Kindersley

**LONDON, NEW YORK, AUCKLAND, DELHI, JOHANNESBURG, MUNICH,
PARIS and SYDNEY**

For a full catalog, visit

DK www.dk.com

Project editor Ian Whitelaw
Art editor Brian Rust
Design assistant Marianna Papachrysanthou
DTP manager Joanna Figg-Latham
Production Eunice Paterson
Managing editor Josephine Buchanan
Senior art editor Neville Graham
Special photography Clive Streeter
Editorial consultant Anthony Wilson, Science Museum, London
US editor Charles A. Wills
US consultant Harvey B. Loomis

This Eyewitness ® Book has been conceived by
Dorling Kindersley Limited and Editions Gallimard

© 1992 Dorling Kindersley Limited
This edition © 2000 Dorling Kindersley Limited
First American edition, 1999

Published in the United States by
Dorling Kindersley Publishing, Inc.
375 Hudson Street,
New York, NY 10014
4 6 8 10 9 7 5 3

Dorling Kindersley books are available at special discounts for bulk
purchases for sales promotions or premiums. Special editions, including
personalized covers, excerpts of existing guides, and corporate imprints can be
created in large quantities for specific needs. For more information, contact
Special Markets Dept., Dorling Kindersley Publishing, Inc.

Library of Congress Cataloging-in-Publication Data
Lafferty, Peter.
Force and motion / written by Peter Lafferty.
p. cm. — (Eyewitness Books)
Includes index.
Summary: Explores the principles of force and motion, describing
how they have been applied from ancient to modern times.
1. Force and energy—Juvenile literature.
2. Motion—Juvenile literature. [1. Force and energy. 2. Motion.]
I. Title. II. Title: Force and motion. III. Series.
QC73.4.L34 2000 531—dc20
92-6927
CIP
AC

ISBN 0-7894-6181-1 (pb)
ISBN 0-7894-4882-3 (hc)

Color reproduction by Colourscan, Singapore
Printed in China by Toppan Printing Co. (Shenzhen) Ltd.

Replica of a simple
Roman crane
powered by a
treadwheel

Joule's apparatus
for determining
the mechanical
equivalent of heat

Contents

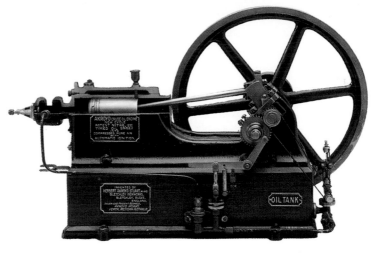

Model of the Akroyd crude oil engine designed by
Herbert Akroyd Stuart and patented in 1890

The world in motion

THE WORLD AROUND US is never still. In the towns, cars and trucks move along the streets. Above the countryside, aircraft fly through the sky. Obviously, such machines are driven by their engines. Their engines are complex machines that produce a force – a push or a pull – to drive the vehicle along. But how do machines produce their power and how do forces produce movements? And what about the movement of natural objects and phenomena? Why do winds blow and rivers flow? Why do the sun and the moon move across the sky? Are all moving objects pulled or pushed along by forces? These questions have been asked for thousands of years. Ancient Greek thinkers such as Aristotle thought they had the answers, but later scientists proved them wrong. Over the centuries scientists such as Galileo, Newton, and Einstein have investigated the world around us and discovered that it is a far more wonderful and mysterious place than even Aristotle imagined.

Flames and smoke rise into the air from a raging forest fire

Water cascades down a rockface in the Atlas Mountains in Morocco

THE FOUR ELEMENTS
Aristotle, who was born in northern Greece in 384 BC and died in 322 BC, studied with Plato and later taught Alexander the Great. From his study of the natural world he concluded that there were four basic forms of matter, called elements: solid earth, fluid water, gaseous air, and hot fire. He believed that if they were left to themselves, the elements would move to their natural places: air bubbles rise through water; fire rises through air; earth sinks through water. Forces were produced by elements striving to find their natural places. It was air and fire struggling to rise through the earth that produced earthquakes and volcanoes.

The earth's crust is torn apart as a volcano releases fire and gas from below the ground

Banks of cloud are sent flying across the sky by strong winds

THE CRYSTAL SPHERES
This statue represents Atlas, the legendary Greek Titan, holding up the earth on his shoulders. The question of how the earth, the sun, and the planets are supported and what causes them to move across the skies has troubled thinkers since ancient times. In his book *Meteorology*, Aristotle explained that water, air, and fire form spherical shells around the earth. Above these was a set of transparent spheres that held the stars and planets as they revolved. The spheres were thought to be made of a rigid, clear material like crystal, which was not subject to the laws that govern the behavior of the earthly elements. This was why the stars and planets could move without a force acting on them. On earth an object could move only if it was acted upon by a force. The movement would stop if this force was removed.

Assyrian sculpture c. 650 BC
showing soldiers carried by
mule-drawn chariot

Greek athletes
throwing discus
and javelin

GREATER FORCE
The Greeks knew that humans were
weak in comparison to the natural
forces that can be seen all around us.
They looked for ways of increasing
human power and of harnessing the
forces of nature. These are tasks that
can be performed by simple machines.
Machines are devices that magnify
forces or allow forces to be used in
new ways. The chariot wheel and the
axle allow a horse to carry a larger
number of people. The bow can shoot an
arrow farther than a javelin can be thrown.
The sailing ship harnesses the wind and
makes it possible to travel farther and faster.

Persian archer shooting an arrow

Greek trireme powered
by oarsmen or sails

7

Ramps and wedges

How did the Ancient Egyptians raise huge blocks of stone to build the pyramids? Surprisingly, the answer is that they used machines – not complicated ones with wheels and gears and shafts, but machines so simple that they don't even look like machines. All machines deal with forces, increasing the usefulness of forces. Some machines transmit forces from one place to another. Others magnify forces, so that a small effort can produce a large effect. No one is sure exactly how the Egyptians moved the huge stone blocks to build the pyramids, but they must have used a simple machine – probably the ramp, or inclined plane. They may have built ramps from the ground around the rising pyramid and dragged the blocks up the slope. This was easier than lifting the blocks straight up – the force needed to drag a block along a perfectly smooth slope is less than the weight (p. 34) of the block. However, it must be dragged farther to achieve the same lift.

THE ZIG-ZAG ROUTE
A winding mountain road is a simple machine that makes it easier for vehicles to travel up a slope by turning back and forth across the mountainside.

Spiral ramp

PYRAMID BUILDING
A spiral ramp winds its way around a pyramid, like a road winding up a mountain. A spiral ramp is longer and more gradual than a ramp going directly up the side of the pyramid. This means that less effort is needed to lift the building blocks. Of course, the blocks have to be dragged much farther, around the pyramid many times, to reach the top.

THE ADVANTAGE OF MACHINES
On the far right, four workers struggle to lift a stone block directly into position. Meanwhile, assuming that there is no frictional force (p. 38), a single worker can accomplish the same task by dragging the block up a ramp. Although the load is the same in each case, the effort required is less using the ramp. It has allowed a small effort force (the pull of a single worker) to overcome a larger load force (the weight of the stone). The ramp is said to give a "mechanical advantage" since it magnifies the effort force. This perfectly smooth ramp allows one worker to accomplish what it normally takes four workers to do, so the mechanical advantage is four. The reason for this is that the ramp is four times as long as its height, and the single worker is having to drag his load four times as far. Increasing the distance moved reduces the effort needed, but the task will take longer to complete.

Wedge-shaped blade

BRONZE AGE AXE HEAD
The inclined plane appears in many guises. The most common form is as a wedge. An axe is a sharp wedge fitted to a handle. While the ramp allows a weight to be raised, the axe head allows a small force – swinging the axe – to produce a strong cutting or splitting force as the blade moves between the two surfaces being split apart. A doorstop works in the same way, forcing the floor and the door apart and jamming the door in position. The cutting blades of knives and scissors are also wedges, forcing apart the material being cut.

Load

Effort applied up the ramp

Ramp

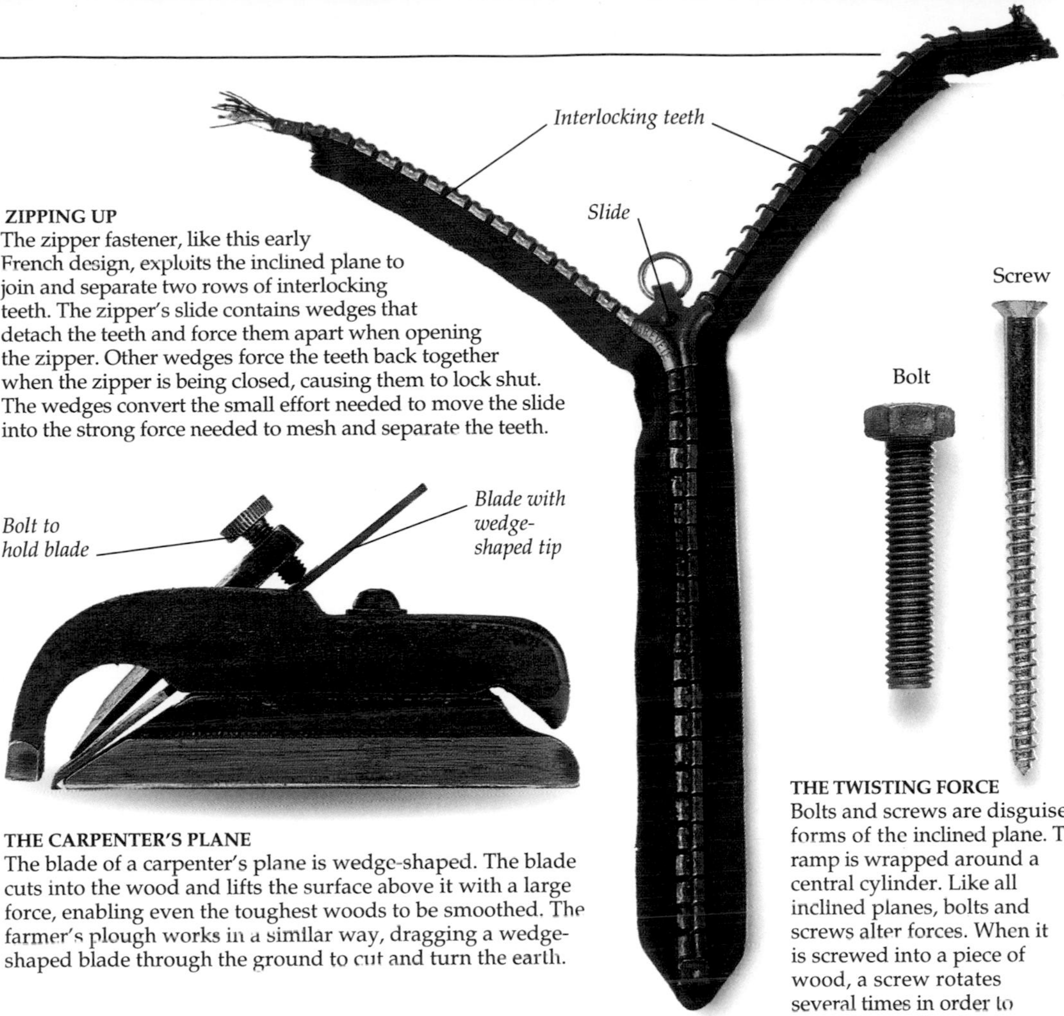

ZIPPING UP

The zipper fastener, like this early French design, exploits the inclined plane to join and separate two rows of interlocking teeth. The zipper's slide contains wedges that detach the teeth and force them apart when opening the zipper. Other wedges force the teeth back together when the zipper is being closed, causing them to lock shut. The wedges convert the small effort needed to move the slide into the strong force needed to mesh and separate the teeth.

Interlocking teeth

Slide

Screw

Bolt

Bolt to hold blade

Blade with wedge-shaped tip

Effort

Downward motion produces sideways force, splitting wood apart

Wedge

Log

THE CARPENTER'S PLANE

The blade of a carpenter's plane is wedge-shaped. The blade cuts into the wood and lifts the surface above it with a large force, enabling even the toughest woods to be smoothed. The farmer's plough works in a similar way, dragging a wedge-shaped blade through the ground to cut and turn the earth.

THE TWISTING FORCE

Bolts and screws are disguised forms of the inclined plane. The ramp is wrapped around a central cylinder. Like all inclined planes, bolts and screws alter forces. When it is screwed into a piece of wood, a screw rotates several times in order to move forward a short distance. Hence it pulls into the wood with a greater force than is used to turn it.

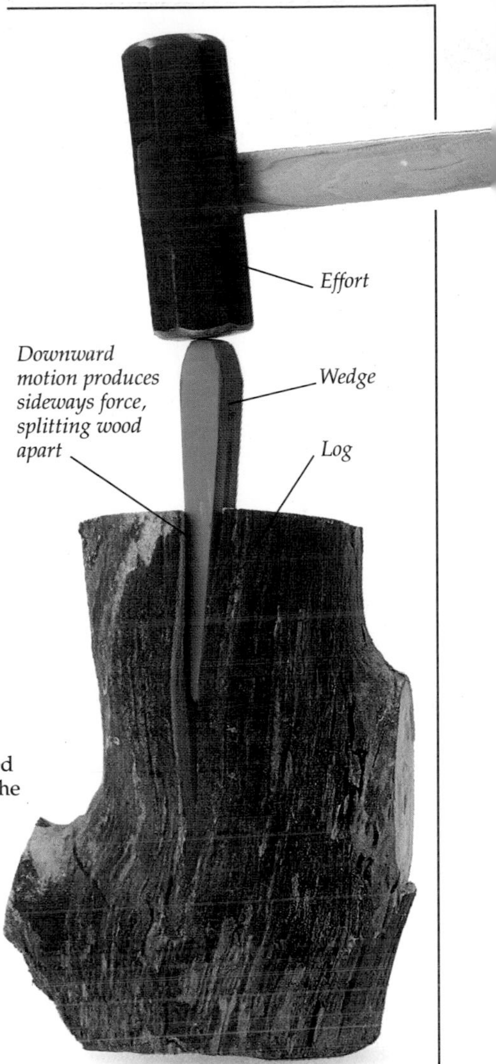

SPLITTING WOOD

A wedge can split wood because it converts a downward movement into a sideways force that splits the wood apart. Because the wood is forced apart by only a small amount when the wedge moves down by a large amount, the forces involved are not equal. The sideways force is much more powerful than the force needed to push the wedge into the wood.

Effort applied vertically

Load

Wheels and axles

THE WHEEL IS A VERY ANCIENT INVENTION and a very useful one, with more uses than just transportation. When it revolves around a central axle, the wheel becomes a machine that can transmit and magnify forces. As in any machine, a small force moving a large distance can produce a large force moving a small distance. If a wheel is turned by a small force at its rim, a larger force will be generated at the axle. Waterwheels and capstans are obvious examples, but there are many others, such as a round door handle or a water faucet.

POTTER'S WHEEL
This 1822 picture shows an Indian potter pushing a wheel around with his foot to produce a turning force at the axle, where the clay is being worked.

HARD AT WORK
Early industry relied upon a few simple machines, such as levers, pulleys, and wheels. This medieval painting shows a man-powered treadmill in the shape of a wheel being used to lift building materials up a tower under construction.

WATER POWER
This waterwheel was in use in the early 19th century to provide power to drive machinery in a cotton mill in Lancashire, England. The wheel was 62 ft (19 m) across and produced the same power as 150 horses. Vertical waterwheels proved better than horizontal ones because they could be built larger and could therefore generate more power.

Grain to be milled

Millstone

THE GREEK MILL
The earliest waterwheels, used to grind grain in Greece during the first century BC, had a horizontal paddle wheel. Like all waterwheels, they act as a wheel and axle, with the force pressing on the paddles at the rim producing a stronger force at the central axle.

Milled flour

Water supply

Axle

Horizontal paddle is pushed around by water pressure

HAUL AWAY

The capstan was used for many centuries to haul up the anchor of a ship. Turned by sailors pushing on the long arms, the capstan acts as a wheel and axle, magnifying the turning force. The anchor is lifted by a rope or chain winding around the central axle. The arms on this 1820 capstan can be removed so that it takes up less room on deck when not in use. A ratchet in the base of the capstan prevents it from turning back and allowing the anchor to fall.

Arm on which pressure is applied

Rope is hauled in

Ratchet mechanism

Central axle

THE CAPSTAN ON LAND

The capstan, or windlass, can also be used to move loads on land. This 19th-century watercolor shows a horse-driven windlass being used to haul up coal from an underground mine by means of ropes that run over pulleys (p. 18) at the top of the shaft.

Rolling along

The most common use of the wheel is not as a machine, but as a means of reducing the effect of friction (p. 38), the dragging force between surfaces. As a wheel rolls along, each point along the wheel's rim touches the ground and then rises up, rather than dragging. This makes it easier to move heavy loads over rough surfaces.

SOLID WHEELS

The wheels on this chariot from 2,500 BC, found painted on a stone in the tomb of the kings of Ur in Iraq, are clearly made from two separate planks joined together. Being mounted on axles, wheels remain in position under the load and they are therefore more convenient to use than rollers.

THE SEMI-SOLID WHEEL

In order to reduce weight, heavy solid wooden wheels could be made lighter by cutting out sections and leaving a cross-bar, as this picture of an early Brazilian carriage shows. The spoked wheel developed from wheels like these.

BEFORE THE WHEEL

These Egyptians are using rollers to help drag the giant stone head of a statue. Each roller must repeatedly be carried forward and placed at the front of the heavy load.

Saddle

Spoked wheels

THE HOBBY HORSE

In 1817 the German Baron Karl von Drais produced the forerunner of the bicycle. Like this English version, it consisted of a wooden beam set above two spoked wooden wheels in line. The rider sat astride the saddle, pushing the ground with alternate feet, turning the front wheel to steer. Apart from the true horse, this was the fastest thing on the roads at the time, reaching speeds of up to 10 mph (16 km/h).

Archimedes' screw

ARCHIMEDES WAS ONE OF THE GREATEST engineers and inventors in ancient Greece. He was the first person to make a scientific study of simple machines, and he used his knowledge to build many different machines. His name is associated with the lifting screw, a simple machine in which an inclined plane (p. 10) is wrapped around a shaft inside a tube. Turning the screw causes the inclined plane to act as a wedge that lifts a portion of water. The effort needed to lift the load is reduced, but the screw has to be turned many times to raise the water a short distance. It also takes longer than raising the water vertically by hand.

RUNNING UPHILL
The Archimedean screw is a device for raising water from low-lying rivers or canals. It consists of an inclined plane wrapped around a central pole to form a screw. This kind of spiral is called a helix. This is enclosed in a tube and one end is placed in the river. When a handle at the other end is turned, the screw lifts the water up the tube until it spills out at the top end. The screw is a machine, allowing a small force (the man's effort) to overcome a larger one (the weight of the water). As the screw turns, the full length of the helical plane runs under each pocket of water to raise it the length of the tube, so the water effectively travels a large distance to achieve a small lift. Therefore only a small force is needed to lift it. In fact, additional effort is needed to overcome the friction (p. 38) of the screw rubbing against the sides of the tube.

DRAWING WATER
Italian scientist and artist Leonardo da Vinci (1452-1519) designed this version of the Archimedean screw. The helical surfaces that lift the water are actually helical tubes wound around the shafts. One of the screws consists of three tubes round a triangular shaft. Da Vinci has also illustrated a system of waterwheels (p. 10) to lift water.

Handle is turned to lift water

Water flows out of the tube

Irrigation channel

Wooden tube cut away to show screw

Helical lifting surface

HAUL AWAY

The capstan was used for many centuries to haul up the anchor of a ship. Turned by sailors pushing on the long arms, the capstan acts as a wheel and axle, magnifying the turning force. The anchor is lifted by a rope or chain winding around the central axle. The arms on this 1820 capstan can be removed so that it takes up less room on deck when not in use. A ratchet in the base of the capstan prevents it from turning back and allowing the anchor to fall.

Arm on which pressure is applied

Rope is hauled in

Ratchet mechanism

Central axle

THE CAPSTAN ON LAND
The capstan, or windlass, can also be used to move loads on land. This 19th-century watercolor shows a horse-driven windlass being used to haul up coal from an underground mine by means of ropes that run over pulleys (p. 18) at the top of the shaft.

Rolling along

The most common use of the wheel is not as a machine, but as a means of reducing the effect of friction (p. 38), the dragging force between surfaces. As a wheel rolls along, each point along the wheel's rim touches the ground and then rises up, rather than dragging. This makes it easier to move heavy loads over rough surfaces.

SOLID WHEELS
The wheels on this chariot from 2,500 BC, found painted on a stone in the tomb of the kings of Ur in Iraq, are clearly made from two separate planks joined together. Being mounted on axles, wheels remain in position under the load and they are therefore more convenient to use than rollers.

THE SEMI-SOLID WHEEL
In order to reduce weight, heavy solid wooden wheels could be made lighter by cutting out sections and leaving a cross-bar, as this picture of an early Brazilian carriage shows. The spoked wheel developed from wheels like these.

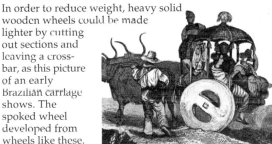

BEFORE THE WHEEL
These Egyptians are using rollers to help drag the giant stone head of a statue. Each roller must repeatedly be carried forward and placed at the front of the heavy load.

Saddle

Spoked wheels

THE HOBBY HORSE
In 1817 the German Baron Karl von Drais produced the forerunner of the bicycle. Like this English version, it consisted of a wooden beam set above two spoked wooden wheels in line. The rider sat astride the saddle, pushing the ground with alternate feet, turning the front wheel to steer. Apart from the true horse, this was the fastest thing on the roads at the time, reaching speeds of up to 10 mph (16 km/h).

Archimedes' screw

ARCHIMEDES WAS ONE OF THE GREATEST engineers and inventors in ancient Greece. He was the first person to make a scientific study of simple machines, and he used his knowledge to build many different machines. His name is associated with the lifting screw, a simple machine in which an inclined plane (p. 10) is wrapped around a shaft inside a tube. Turning the screw causes the inclined plane to act as a wedge that lifts a portion of water. The effort needed to lift the load is reduced, but the screw has to be turned many times to raise the water a short distance. It also takes longer than raising the water vertically by hand.

RUNNING UPHILL

The Archimedean screw is a device for raising water from low-lying rivers or canals. It consists of an inclined plane wrapped around a central pole to form a screw. This kind of spiral is called a helix. This is enclosed in a tube and one end is placed in the river. When a handle at the other end is turned, the screw lifts the water up the tube until it spills out at the top end. The screw is a machine, allowing a small force (the man's effort) to overcome a larger one (the weight of the water). As the screw turns, the full length of the helical plane runs under each pocket of water to raise it the length of the tube, so the water effectively travels a large distance to achieve a small lift. Therefore only a small force is needed to lift it. In fact, additional effort is needed to overcome the friction (p. 38) of the screw rubbing against the sides of the tube.

Handle is turned to lift water

Water flows out of the tube

DRAWING WATER
Italian scientist and artist Leonardo da Vinci (1452-1519) designed this version of the Archimedean screw. The helical surfaces that lift the water are actually helical tubes wound around the shafts. One of the screws consists of three tubes round a triangular shaft. Da Vinci has also illustrated a system of waterwheels (p. 10) to lift water.

Wooden tube cut away to show screw

Helical lifting surface

Irrigation channel

RAISING GRAIN

The Archimedean screw finds a place today on the farm. When a combine harvester has cut the crop and separated the grain from the chaff (the straw and the husks), a rotating screw, or auger, carries the grain up a tube. It then flows out of the top into a waiting truck. Similar augers are used in bakeries and factories to move flour and other fine powders that behave rather like liquids.

Ratchet

Handle

Auger bit

THE MINER'S ROCK-DRILL

This kind of drill is also called an auger and it is used to drill a hole and remove the loose material. This particular drill is used to cut holes in rock so that explosives can be inserted. As the drill is turned, its double-bladed cutting tip bites into the rock and earth, breaking away small pieces. This waste material is carried out of the deepening hole along the grooves of the drill bit, in the same way that water is lifted up the Archimedean screw. Large augers are used to make holes in soft ground to insert the foundations for tall buildings.

CURLING SWARF

When a drill bit cuts through soft metal, the waste metal, or swarf, that the drill cuts out takes the form of a helix. This demonstrates the similarity between the Archimedean screw, the auger, and the spiral staircase. The stairs are more accurately called a "helical staircase."

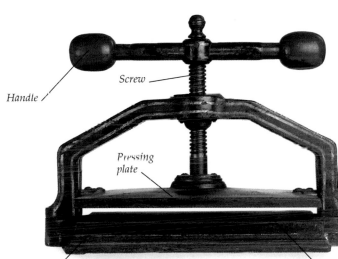

Handle

Screw

Pressing plate

Base plate

PRESSING DOWN

An early use for the screw was in the simple printing press. A screw was used to force down a plate that pressed a sheet of paper on to a tray of inked metal letters, or type. The small force needed to turn the handle produces a far greater force pressing down on the paper. This press was used for making copies of letters. Similar presses were also used to stamp coins out of soft metals.

Paper inserted here

Helical swarf   Drill bit

TAKING THE LONG WAY AROUND

Walking up a spiral staircase from the bottom to the top is easier than climbing the same height up a vertical ladder, even though the distance walked is much greater. This is because the slope of the winding stairs is far less steep. This is similar to Archimedes' screw, which winds around and around in order to raise the water a small distance.

Sharpened drill tip

Water source

Fixing post holds the tube in place

Floating and sinking

THE GREEK SCIENTIST Archimedes is best known for his "Principle." This explains why some objects float and some objects sink in liquids. Objects that are full of air, such as a hollow ball, are good floaters. But it is not just air-filled objects that float. Many solid objects, such as apples, also float. Archimedes' first insight was that all floating objects are supported by an upward force, called buoyancy, or upthrust. The upthrust is caused by the liquid pressing against the floating object. The upthrust can be felt if a table tennis ball is pushed under water. This is the force that makes things float. Archimedes' second insight was that the force of the upthrust on an object depends on how much liquid the object pushes aside, or displaces. If an object displaces enough liquid, it experiences an upthrust strong enough to support its weight, and the object floats. After many experiments, Archimedes discovered that the amount of upthrust on a floating object is equal to the weight of the liquid it displaces. This is called Archimedes' Principle.

Spring balance

Apple being weighed

1 WEIGHING
An object that will float – in this case an apple – is weighed on a spring balance and its weight is recorded.

2 FLOATING AND BALANCING
Two identical beakers are then placed in the pans of an accurate set of scales (right). The two beakers are filled to the brim with water and the scales are seen to balance. The apple is now lowered into the right-hand beaker until it floats. The water that overflows is carefully caught. When the apple has settled, it is found that the scales are still balanced.

Testing the theory
This three-part experiment puts Archimedes' principle to the test by comparing the weight of a floating object with the weight of the liquid that it displaces. The principle that the upthrust on an object is equal to the weight of liquid that it displaces also applies to objects that do not float, but in these cases the upthrust is less than the weight of the object, which therefore sinks. Archimedes realized that a sinking object displaces a volume of liquid equal to its own volume, and he used this fact to help King Hieron find out whether his crown was pure gold.

Beaker full of water

Scale pan

FLOATING BALLS
Three balls of the same size – a table tennis ball (left), a rubber squash ball (center), and a hardwood ball (right) – float in water. Each ball sinks until it displaces enough water to produce an upthrust equal to its weight. The table tennis ball is light and so sinks little. The hardwood ball weighs the most. It sinks until it is almost underwater.

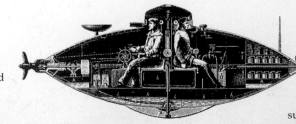

UNDER THE WAVES
A submarine, such as this 1881 Russian model, submerges because it takes water into its tanks. This increases the weight of the boat and, since the upthrust is unchanged, the submarine sinks. To make it rise, water is pumped out of the tanks.

Arm of weighing balance

"EUREKA!"

Archimedes is said to have discovered his Principle on seeing the water rise as he got into his bath. King Hieron had asked him to find out whether the King's new crown was pure gold, without damaging it. At the palace he lowered the crown into a jug of water and noted how far the water rose. He then did the same with a piece of pure gold of the same weight and the water rose by less, proving that the crown contained another, less dense metal.

Full beaker with apple floating in it

Scale pan

FLOATING ON AIR

Albert and Gaston Tissandier, French aeronauts, made a trial run in their rigid airship, or dirigible, in 1883. The airship was filled with hydrogen gas, which is less dense than air, so the upthrust of the air on the airship was greater than the ship's weight.

HOT AIR

The hot air inside a balloon is less dense than the colder air that surrounds it. The balloon will stay aloft as long as the air inside it is kept warm.

Spring balance

Water being weighed

3 WEIGHING THE WATER

When the water that overflowed from the beaker is weighed (right), this displaced water is found to weigh precisely the same as the apple. The reason that the scales still balance is that the apple has displaced exactly the weight of water that compensates for the addition of the weight of the apple to the pan. Because the apple floats, the upthrust must be equal to the weight of the apple. The spring balance has shown this to be the same as the weight of the water displaced. So Archimedes was right – the size of the upthrust on the apple equals the weight of the water displaced.

MEASURING DENSITY

The hydrometer is an instrument used to measure the density of liquids. It is used in the brewing industry, for example, to measure the density of alcoholic drinks. The instrument consists of a glass tube that floats upright, sinking deeply into less dense liquids such as denatured alcohol (below) and floating high in dense liquids such as glycerin (far right).

Hydrometer in glycerin

Hydrometer in water

Hydrometer in denatured alcohol

STAYING BUOYANT

Bony fishes have an air-filled sac, called a swim bladder, inside their bodies. The pressure of the air in the swim bladder is adjusted to maintain buoyancy at different depths of water. By compressing the air in the bladder, the fish can sink down in the water.

Levers

A LEVER IS A simple machine. It consists of a rigid bar which can turn around a fixed point, called the fulcrum. A crowbar is a kind of lever, and it is used as a force magnifier to lift heavy weights by using smaller forces. The load, at one end of the bar, is overcome by a smaller force, the effort, applied at the other end. Such a lever is said to have a positive "mechanical advantage." To achieve this, the lever must obey the rule that applies to all force magnifiers: the effort must move a greater distance than the load. To raise a heavy rock, the effort applied at the end of the bar must move farther than the rock rises.

Studying levers

This apparatus was made during the 1700s to show the action of the lever. The lever is the horizontal beam resting upon, or held down by, the fulcrum at the top of the upright on the left. The "load" consists of a weight hung below the lever, and the "effort" force is provided by another weight hanging over the upper pulley. The positions of the load and effort can be changed to demonstrate the three different classes of lever.

Effort

Lever

Fulcrum

Load

CLASS 2 LEVER
In a class 2 lever, the load lies between the fulcrum and the effort force. This kind of lever is always a force magnifier, having a good mechanical advantage. In the setup shown here, the two small weights over the pulley are the effort, and the larger load hangs below the center of the lever. Since the load is twice the size of the effort that is supporting it, the mechanical advantage is two.

Effort

Fulcrum

Load

THE CROWBAR – A CLASS 1 LEVER
After a study of levers, Archimedes boasted "Give me a long enough lever and a place to stand, and I will move the earth." Of course, to operate his lever he would have needed a fulcrum, and the artist of this old drawing has kindly provided a conical rock. Archimedes is using a crowbar, a typical class 1 lever, which has the fulcrum between the load and the effort. For greatest mechanical advantage, the load (the earth) must be close to the fulcrum and the lever must be long. During his study of levers, Archimedes discovered the "law of the lever": for balance, the effort multiplied by its distance from the fulcrum must equal the load multiplied by its distance from the fulcrum.

CLASS 3 LEVER
In a class 3 lever, the effort is applied between the fulcrum and the load. Such a lever is a force reducer, since the effort (the single large weight) is greater than the load (the two small weights), and its mechanical advantage is therefore less than one. In this case the effort is pulling up against the fulcrum rather than resting on top of it. The human arm is a class 3 lever with the elbow as the fulcrum.

SWEET AND STRONG

These 19th-century sugar nippers are a pair of class 1 levers joined in the middle. Each arm turns around the central hinge or fulcrum. The effort is applied to the ends held in the hand. The load consists of a lump of sugar between the cutting blades. These nippers were used to break off chunks from a sugar loaf for cooking or to sweeten coffee or tea. Modern scissors work in the same way.

ROCK-A-BYE BABY

A seesaw is a class 1 lever with a central fulcrum. It is designed to balance and to produce no mechanical advantage. Children of equal weights should therefore sit at the ends of the seesaw, but if the weights are unequal, the heavier child should sit nearer to the fulcrum.

THE LEVER AT WAR

The trebuchet, a medieval war machine for hurling large rocks, used a class 1 lever. When the heavy weight at one end is dropped, it levers the longer arm swiftly around and launches a rock from the rope bag at the other end of it.

Load

Effort

Fulcrum

Effort

Fulcrum

CRACKING FORCE

Nutcrackers are a pair of class 2 levers sharing a fulcrum at one end. The effort is applied at the ends of the levers, or arms, squeezing the nut held in the middle, which is the load. Class 2 levers can be powerful force magnifiers – in this case enabling the effort of a hand to crack the toughest nut.

Load

ON THE FIDDLE

As the giant pincer of the fiddler crab is a class 3 lever, the muscle that pulls the pincer shut has to be extremely strong to produce the force that the crab needs.

A MEAL OF RICE AND FISH

Chopsticks are class 3 levers and are therefore force reducers. They do not grip the food strongly, but they are able to magnify movements. Small motions of the fingers are converted into longer, though weaker, movements at the tips of the chopsticks.

AGE-OLD DESIGN

As this medieval painting shows, the design of the wheel barrow has not changed in centuries, as it is ideal for moving heavy loads by hand. It is a class 2 lever, with the load being placed between the effort and the fulcrum. Lifting the handles with a light effort raises a heavy load closer to the fulcrum, which is the axle (p. 10) of the wheel on which the barrow rolls.

A TOOL FROM ANCIENT ROME

These bronze Roman scissors, once used for cutting cloth, are a pair of class 3 levers. The blades turn about the hinge at one end, and the user squeezes the blades together in the middle. The load is the resistance of the cloth. These scissors require a greater effort than modern ones, but they are still used by sheep shearers, as the blades open wide to take in the thick fleece.

Fulcrum   *Effort*   *Load*

Hoist away

According to legend, King Hieron of Syracuse once challenged Archimedes to drag a large ship up the beach singlehandedly. Archimedes studied the problem and decided upon the best machine for the task – a pulley. A pulley is a machine in which a rope passes back and forth over one or more grooved wheels. One end of the rope is attached to the load and the other end is pulled in order to move or lift the load. Simple pulleys have only one wheel. These pulleys change the direction in which a force acts, but they do not magnify forces. Compound pulleys – pulleys with more than one wheel – are able to magnify forces. Archimedes attached to the ship a compound pulley, composed of many pulley wheels, and he was able to drag the ship up the shore without help. Like the ramp and the lever, the pulley allows a small effort to overcome a large load because the effort moves through a greater distance than the load. In a pulley system comprising two wheels, the effort will move twice as far as the load, giving a mechanical advantage of two, but friction (p. 38) and the weight of the pulleys reduce the advantage.

Load, including weight of the lower pulley

Effort

THE POWER OF THE PULLEY
Making use of the same effort, different pulley systems will support different loads. On the right is a simple pulley in which the weights on both ends of the string are equal. There is no force magnification. The compound pulley system on the left consists of two triple wheels with the string passing over all six wheels. Using this system, the load is much greater than the weight that is lifting it. This system magnifies the lifting force by six times (assuming that there is no friction), although this is not immediately apparent since the weight of the lower pulley must be considered as part of the load. The middle pulleys magnify the lifting force by four and two times. The theoretical mechanical advantage of a pulley system – how much the system magnifies a force – is the same as the number of strands of rope supporting the lower wheel. This advantage is gained at the price of having to pull the end of the rope farther than the load rises.

THE PULLEY AT WAR
A medieval bowman loads his crossbow by winding a handle attached to a double pulley that pulls back the string. A crossbow bolt could pierce armor, but to achieve this power the string had to be under great tension, and a large force was therefore needed to load it.

THE PULLEY AT WORK
Five men pull a rope that passes over a simple pulley, raising a weight, which is then allowed to drop on to a pile, driving it into the ground. The pulley makes the work lighter since it is easier to pull a rope down than to lift a weight up.

Rotating cabin mounted on steel rollers

145-ton counterweight

100-foot-long hull

FLOATING CRANE

Seen here as a cutaway model, this crane was built in 1886 for use at the Tilbury Docks on the River Thames near London. The crane has a lifting capacity of 60 tons and is mounted on a floating platform. The tubular steel boom, strengthened by a wrought iron framework, is 92 ft (28 m) long and rests on a 26 ft (8 m) diameter circle of steel rollers. The rollers are supported on an iron cylinder built into the hull. The crane's lifting tackle consists of a compound pulley system through which the cable runs. The cable is raised and lowered by a hoisting drum powered by a two-cylinder engine. Inside the cabin, the weight of the boom and the load is counterbalanced by a wrought iron truck weighing 145 tons. This counterbalance truck runs on rails and can be moved back and forth to achieve the best balance.

Three-wheeled pulley

MAN-POWERED CRANE

A medieval painting shows a single pulley in one of its most common roles – on the end of a simple crane. The crane, at the top of a tower under construction, is being used to raise building materials. It is powered by two unfortunate individuals in a treadwheel. As they walk, the treadwheel turns, and this draws in or plays out the rope, which is attached to the lifting basket. Single pulleys do not offer a mechanical advantage, but they have the useful quality of changing the direction in which a force is acting.

Wrought iron supporting member

Lifting cables

Three-wheeled pulley

Tubular steel boom member

Cannon being lifted

Hoisting drum driven by a two-cylinder motor

ARCHIMEDES REVISITED

In a scene from the movie *Fitzcarraldo*, this ship is being dragged up a steep slope in the Andes Mountains in South America using an elaborate system of pulleys. The ship's own power is being used to haul on the cables. This scene echoes the story of Archimedes' accomplishment at Syracuse when he moved a ship singlehandedly.

PULLEY-OPERATED ELEVATOR

A 19th-century design for a water-powered elevator shows pulleys being used in two ways. A strong cable runs from the roof of the elevator car, up over a pulley wheel and down to another pulley wheel. This is attached to a piston that slides up and down in a tube. The piston is driven from above and below by the pressure of water in the tube. A rope passing around a second pair of pulley wheels enables the lift attendant to turn a valve at the base of the shaft, directing water into the top or bottom of the tube, pushing the piston down or up to raise or lower the elevator car.

Getting into gear

GEARS ARE PAIRS of interlocking toothed wheels that transmit force and motion in machines. The four basic kinds of gears are rack and pinion, spur, bevel, and worm gears. In a pair of gear wheels, the smaller wheel turns more quickly than the larger one, and this difference in speed produces a difference in the force transmitted; the larger wheel turns with a greater force. Gears can therefore be used to increase or decrease a force, and to change the speed of a rotation, as well as its direction.

Interlocking teeth

SPUR GEAR
The spur gear consists of two interlocking toothed wheels in the same plane. The gears above are fragments of an ancient calendar instrument, dating from around AD 500, which probably showed the positions of the sun and moon on a dial.

WORM GEAR
The worm gear is a shaft encircled by a screw thread, into which a toothed wheel fits. It can produce a strong force, and it is often used on musical instruments, such as the guitar and double bass, to tighten the strings.

CHANGING DIRECTION
The ancient Romans used wooden bevel-type gears like these in water mills, to change the direction of rotation from horizontal to vertical.

BEVEL GEARS
Bevel gears consist of two toothed wheels that mesh at an angle, altering the direction of the rotation. If the two wheels have different numbers of teeth, they also alter speed and force. For instance, if the big wheel has twice as many teeth, it rotates with half the speed and twice the force of the small wheel.

RACK AND PINION
The rack and pinion gear consists of a toothed wheel, the pinion, which meshes with a toothed sliding rack. It converts a rotary motion into a straight line motion. In this apparatus, moving the diagonal bar up and down raises each plunger in turn to pump out air from below. Rack and pinion gears are also used in the steering systems of some cars to connect the steering column to the front wheels.

BUDDING'S BLADE-RUNNER
Edwin Budding made this, the first lawn mower, in 1830. A series of spur gears connects the main roller to the knife blades, rotating them at 12 times the speed of the roller. A lever operates the clutch to disconnect the gears so that the mower can be moved without the blades being turned.

Clutch lever

Roller

Intermediate gear wheels

Blades

Gear wheel to turn the blades

Driving gear wheel

STEAM-POWERED GEARS
Richard Trevithick, from Cornwall in England, designed and built the very first steam locomotive in 1803. This is the original drawing of his improved version, built in 1805. In both engines the back-and-forth motion of the piston was made to turn the wheels by an arrangement of spur gears. His first locomotive was tested at a coal mine in South Wales, where it hauled five wagons and 70 men a distance of 9 miles (15 km) at a speed of nearly 5 mph (8 km/h).

Cutting blade

Semi-circular rack

Spur gear

Handle

KITCHEN GEAR
This 1863 fruit and vegetable peeling machine uses a rack and pinion to drive spur gears that turn an apple against a cutting blade. As the handle is pushed around the semicircular base, the peel is removed from the apple in a single sweep.

Pinion

JAMES WATT
The great British engineer James Watt (1736-1819) developed the first efficient steam engine, one of the driving forces behind the Industrial Revolution. His engines made use of a kind of spur gear called a sun-and-planet (or epicyclic) gear, which turned the up-and-down motion of the engine piston into a rotary motion to drive an axle. The gears consist of a small "planet" gear that revolves around a larger "sun" gear wheel.

THE GEARED "FACILE" BICYCLE
Early bicycles often had a very large front wheel, so that a single turn of the pedals would carry the rider a long way. The large wheel also gave a smoother ride. One bicycle introduced in the 1870s had a front wheel 5 ft (1.5 m) tall and a back wheel only two-fifths as large. Unfortunately, these bicycles were dangerous to ride – if the bicycle stopped suddenly, the rider was thrown over the handlebars. This Facile bicycle, produced in 1888, was safer because there was less difference in the size of the two wheels. The pedals are connected to the front wheel by sun-and-planet gearing, converting the up-and-down movement of the pedals into rotation of the wheel.

Pedal driving planet gear, which runs around the central sun gear to turn the wheel axle

Complex machines

SIMPLE MACHINES ARE the building blocks of complex machines. Even the most complex of machines is made up of levers, gears, pulleys, screws, wheels, and axles. These simple machines are connected together in many ingenious ways to produce printing presses, cars, dental drills, photocopiers, food processors, and so on. The parts of many complex machines are linked by series of gears (gear trains), levers, belts, chains, and transmission shafts. Cranks and cams are also useful, converting a turning motion into a back-and-forth motion – to drive the needle up and down in a sewing machine, for example.

THE MIGHTY MACHINE
Actor Charlie Chaplin feels like a small cog in a large machine in the film *Modern Times*. Many industrial machines dwarf the people that operate them.

Knob to wind up mainspring

Balance wheel driven by hairspring

MACHINERY ON THE FARM
An early steam engine drives a threshing machine by means of a belt drive. Sheaves of wheat are forked into the thresher at the top. Sacks are filled with grain at the front of the machine, and the threshed straw is passed up the elevator at the far end.

KEEPING TIME
A mechanical clock, like this early 1900s pocket watch, consists mainly of trains of gearwheels. One train connects the mainspring to a hairspring (p. 46) which spins a balance wheel back and forth at a regular rate. Another series of gears moves the hands round the clockface at a rate dictated by the vibrations of the hairspring.

INSIDE A 1904 AUTOMOBILE
A complex machine, such as a car, can be understood by dividing it up into groups of related parts called systems. The power to drive the car is provided by the engine. The drive train carries the power from the engine to the driving wheels. It consists of clutch, gearbox, universal joint, drive shaft, differential, and half axles. The braking system slows the car down when necessary. It consists of levers and brake drums, connected by various rods. The steering system enables the driver to turn corners. It consists of the steering wheel and linkages to the front wheels. The cooling system keeps the engine at the correct temperature. Its main part is the radiator. The exhaust system takes the waste gases away from the engine through the muffler.

Gearbox controls the speed of the wheels in relation to the speed of the engine

Suspension spring

Half axle

Battery

Differential allows wheels to turn at different rates when cornering

Hand brake

Universal joint

Exhaust pipe

Muffler

Drive shaft

Brake drum

Chassis

Gear lever

Steering wheel

Brake rod

THE MATHEMATICAL MACHINE

The earliest automatic calculator was assembled in 1832 by the English mathematician and engineer Charles Babbage. It consisted of nearly 2,000 levers, cams, and gears, and was one of the finest examples of precision engineering of the time. Called the Difference Engine, the device represented numbers by the teeth on the numerous gearwheels. To make a calculation a handle was turned to drive the first column of gears in a connected series. Babbage also designed a bigger machine consisting of 4,000 parts and weighing 3 tons. Difference Engine No. 2 was finally built by engineers at London's Science Museum in 1991, proving that Babbage's complex design ideas really did work.

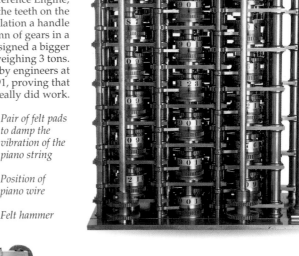

THE WRITER'S FRIEND

This early manual typewriter contains a system of levers that converts a small movement of the fingers on the keys into a long, fast movement of the type bar, which presses an inked ribbon against the paper. On the tip of each type bar there is a lowercase letter and a capital letter. Pressing the "shift" key selects capital letters. Most typewriters have at least five levers between the key and the type bar.

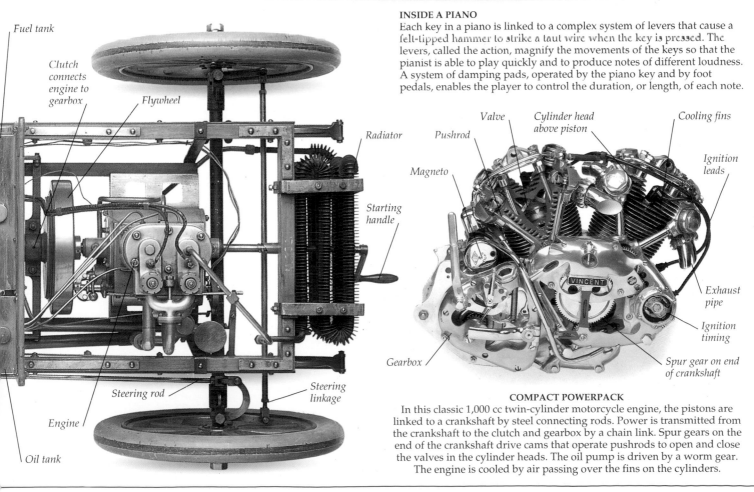

Pair of felt pads to damp the vibration of the piano string

Position of piano wire

Felt hammer

Complex system of levers to control the way the hammer strikes the string

Piano key

Lever to raise damping pads

INSIDE A PIANO

Each key in a piano is linked to a complex system of levers that cause a felt-tipped hammer to strike a taut wire when the key is pressed. The levers, called the action, magnify the movements of the keys so that the pianist is able to play quickly and to produce notes of different loudness. A system of damping pads, operated by the piano key and by foot pedals, enables the player to control the duration, or length, of each note.

Fuel tank

Clutch connects engine to gearbox

Flywheel

Radiator

Starting handle

Valve

Pushrod

Cylinder head above piston

Cooling fins

Magneto

Ignition leads

Exhaust pipe

Ignition timing

Spur gear on end of crankshaft

Gearbox

Steering rod

Steering linkage

Engine

Oil tank

COMPACT POWERPACK

In this classic 1,000 cc twin-cylinder motorcycle engine, the pistons are linked to a crankshaft by steel connecting rods. Power is transmitted from the crankshaft to the clutch and gearbox by a chain link. Spur gears on the end of the crankshaft drive cams that operate pushrods to open and close the valves in the cylinder heads. The oil pump is driven by a worm gear. The engine is cooled by air passing over the fins on the cylinders.

Galileo's science of motion

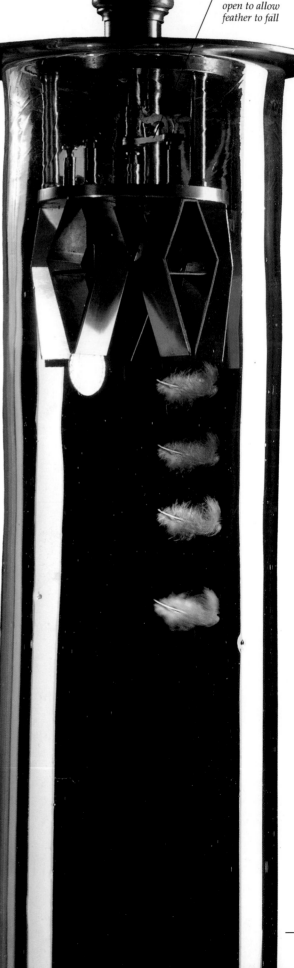

Release mechanism open to allow feather to fall

FOR MORE THAN 1,500 years after Archimedes, science in Europe made little progress. However, new ideas gradually appeared, particularly during the Renaissance, a period of great intellectual activity in Europe from the 1300s to the 1600s. The most important scientist of the late Renaissance was the Italian Galileo Galilei, who was born at Pisa in 1564. He studied the ideas of Archimedes, particularly the use of mathematics to solve physical problems. His study of Archimedes' Principle (p. 14) led him to conclude that all objects would fall at the same speed. This idea was contrary to the teachings of Aristotle, and to prove his point Galileo undertook a series of experiments. His belief in the importance of the experimental approach marks Galileo as one of the first modern scientists and his mathematical description of the way objects fall is still valid today. In 1592 Galileo obtained a post at the University of Padua where he made many discoveries in astronomy using the newly developed telescope. These discoveries conflicted with the teachings of the Roman Catholic Church, and in 1633 Galileo was tried by the Inquisition and forced to deny his findings. He died under house arrest in 1642.

ARISTOTLE DISPROVED (*left*)
According to some stories, Galileo dropped two weights from the top of the leaning tower of Pisa to test his ideas about falling bodies. Aristotle had believed that a heavier weight would hit the ground first, but Galileo found that the two weights hit the ground at about the same time.

IN A VACUUM (*right*)
In this replica of an 18th-century experiment, all the air has been pumped out of the glass tube so that there is no resistance to a falling object. A feather and a golden coin are then released one after the other, and they are found to accelerate at precisely the same rate, as the distances between successive images show.

FALLING SLOWLY
This 19th-century painting shows Galileo demonstrating his ideas by rolling balls down a slope. He reasoned that they would behave in the same way as falling objects – only more slowly. He was able to measure the time they took to fall and found that "the spaces passed over in natural motion are in proportion to the squares of the times."

Release mechanism open to allow the coin to fall

GALILEO'S TRIAL
In 1630 Galileo wrote a book supporting the theory of Polish astronomer Nicolaus Copernicus, who said that the planets, including the earth, revolved around the sun. Galileo was called before the Inquisition to explain why he was questioning traditional beliefs. He was forced to declare that the earth is the immovable center of the universe.

Timing experiments

It was difficult for Galileo to measure short time intervals in his experiments. The very first clock, the sundial, was obviously unsuitable for measuring short time periods. Other simple clocks, such as a sandtimer or candle clock, were also unsuitable for precise scientific work. Mechanical clocks of the time were crude. They were regulated by a small bar that rocked back and forth, and they were inaccurate. Some early mechanical clocks had no dial, but struck a bell each hour. Others had a dial, but with only a single hour hand. Galileo used the human pulse as a simple clock, or measured the amount of water escaping from a jar or funnel to indicate amounts of time. Indeed, the Egyptian water clock was one of the earliest kinds of clock. Galileo did in fact design an accurate pendulum clock but it was not built in his lifetime (p. 46).

SANDS OF TIME
In a sandtimer, fine sand runs down through a narrow hole between two bulbs. Used to show when a fixed period of time has elapsed, it is inadequate for measuring short time intervals.

SIMPLE WATER CLOCK
Galileo may have used a device like this to time his experiments on rolling balls. When a ball is released, the finger is raised from the tube, allowing the water to flow, and when the ball passes a certain point the finger is replaced and the flow of water is stopped. The amount of water collected in the bottle gives a good indication of the time taken.

PENDULUM CLOCK
When he was a young man, Galileo observed that a pendulum always took the same time to swing back and forth. Putting this observation into practice, he later designed a clock that operated on this principle. One of his pupils drew this diagram of the internal workings of the clock, but it was not actually built until the 19th century (p. 46).

The science of the cannonball

GALILEO'S STUDIES OF moving objects (p. 24) brought many insights. He recognized that any force, even a small one, could set an object in motion. In practice, friction (p. 38) prevents objects from being moved by small forces, but if there were no friction, the smallest push or pull would start an object moving. Furthermore, Galileo recognized that once an object was moving it would keep moving until a force halted it. No force was needed to keep an object moving, contrary to Aristotle's teachings that an object would cease to move if the force ceased to act upon it. Galileo went on to study projectiles – objects that are thrown into the air and travel up and along before falling down. A spear, arrow, or cannonball hurled into the air is a projectile. He found that projectiles were moving in two ways at the same time: they were moving forward at a constant speed and moving up and down with a changing speed. The resulting path was a combination of the two motions. Galileo tested his idea by projecting a small ball from the edge of a table and marking the spot where the ball landed.

The path of a projectile, he discovered, was a curve called a "parabola." Galileo had solved a problem that had puzzled kings and warriors ever since gunpowder was invented: how to calculate the flight path of a cannonball.

ARISTOTLE'S FLIGHT PATH
According to Aristotle, the path of any projectile consisted of two straight lines, as seen in this 1561 print. Here a cannonball is shown traveling in a straight line from the cannon and then dropping straight down. Aristotle thought that an object could undertake only one motion at a time.

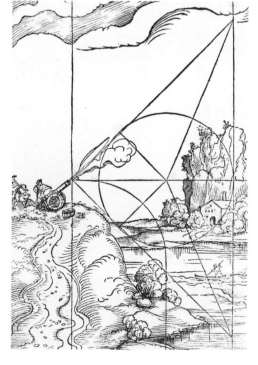

A CIRCULAR PATH
Using a geometrical construction, the artist of this 1547 print drew the path of a cannonball as a circular arc. The ball was thought to begin moving along a straight line, then to move in the arc of a circle, and finally to fall straight down.

COMBINED MOTION
On an apparatus designed to show Galileo's projectile experiment, a ball runs down the curved slope at the top left and is projected from the end of the slope. The ball leaves the slope with a certain horizontal speed, and this is maintained as it falls. This is why the horizontal distances between the images of the falling ball are all equal. The downward, falling motion of the ball is unaffected by the horizontal motion. The increasing vertical distances between the images show that the ball is speeding up, or accelerating, in the normal way for a falling object. The combination of a steady horizontal speed and an accelerating downward motion produces the curved parabolic path. If the ball is projected slightly upward, like a cannonball, its path is a combination of a steady horizontal motion and a changing up-and-down vertical motion.

Curved slope

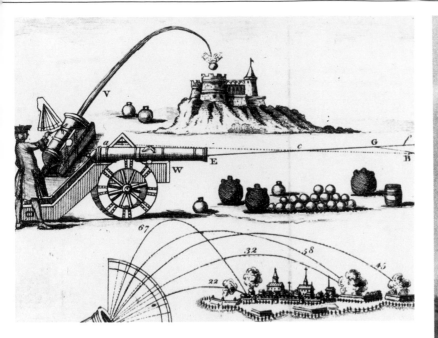

SCIENTIFIC BOMBARDMENT
The paths of the cannonballs in this 18th-century print are shown as parabolas – the correct curve, as Galileo proved. The drawing shows that the maximum range is achieved when the cannon is elevated to 45°. Even today, gunners use computations similar to these to calculate the elevation and direction of artillery fire. Every factor that might affect the flight of the shell is taken into account: distance to target, wind, temperature, air pressure, and even the spin (pp. 46 and 54) of the earth.

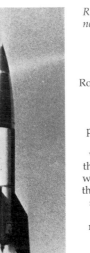

Ring around nose cone

Whistle

BALLISTIC MAIL
Rockets were used to carry messages during World War I (1914-1918). The body of the rocket was packed with gunpowder, which launched it on its way. The nose contained the message and a whistle which shrieked to warn of the rocket's approach. The size of the flange around the nose altered the air resistance and controlled the length of the flight.

THE BALLISTIC ROCKET
A German V2 rocket from World War II (1939-1945) takes off. These rockets carried an explosive warhead and had a range of about 190 miles (300 km), reaching a height of about 60 miles (100 km) under power and then falling freely in a parabolic curve at several times the speed of sound.

End of slope

← *Constant horizontal speed* →

Increasing vertical distances indicate acceleration due to gravity, unaffected by the horizontal motion of the ball

Newton's clockwork universe

ISAAC NEWTON, BORN IN 1642, just a few months after the death of Galileo, was one of the greatest scientists of all time. In the words of the poet Alexander Pope, "Nature, and Nature's Laws lay hid in Night: God said Let Newton be! and All was Light." Isaac Newton extended Galileo's work, admitting himself that "If I have seen further it is by standing on the shoulders of giants" – paying a compliment to Galileo and others who made the discoveries on which he was able to build. Newton's achievement was to bring together the significant discoveries made up until his time and to combine them into a unified picture of the universe. According to Newton, the universe ran like a clockwork machine governed by a few simple laws. Like Galileo, Newton realized that mathematics was the language of science, and he formulated these universal laws of motion and gravitation mathematically. They describe how objects move when they are acted upon by forces.

EARLY LIFE
Isaac Newton was born in the manor house at Woolsthorpe in Lincolnshire, England. His father had died two months earlier, and when Isaac was three his mother remarried. Isaac was then brought up by his grandmother. A quiet, lonely child, he was not interested in the family farm, so in 1661 was sent to study at nearby Cambridge University. During 1665 and 1666, while spending time back at the family home, Newton made many of his most important discoveries.

TRINITY COLLEGE, CAMBRIDGE
In 1669 Newton was appointed Professor of Mathematics at Cambridge, and he remained there until after the publication of his great work, the *Principia*, in 1687. His rooms at Trinity College (below) are situated at the front right of this picture, and he probably had a small laboratory in the gardens outside his rooms.

Moon

Earth

Disc indicating time around the globe

Sun

THE CLOCKWORK UNIVERSE
This clockwork model of the solar system, with the sun in the center orbited by the earth and the moon, was built in about 1712 by John Rowley of London. It is called an orrery after the fourth Earl of Orrery, for whom it was made, and it reflects Newton's view of the universe as a giant machine. The orrery shows the earth's changing position throughout the year. In the Newtonian view, if the position and velocity of every particle in the universe and the size and direction of the forces acting upon them were known, all the future positions and movements of all the particles could be calculated using his laws.

Pointer indicating the earth's progress through the signs of the zodiac in the course of a year

AN ECCENTRIC MAN

In 1701 Newton resigned his position at Cambridge when he was elected as a Member of Parliament. By this time, Newton had become secretive and argumentative, quarrelling with many of his scientific colleagues, and his interests had widened to include such fields as religion and alchemy, as this page from his notebook shows. In 1705 Newton was honored with a knighthood, and after his death in 1727 he was buried in London's Westminster Abbey

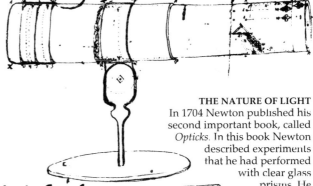

THE NATURE OF LIGHT

In 1704 Newton published his second important book, called *Opticks*. In this book Newton described experiments that he had performed with clear glass prisms. He showed that white light is made up of all the colors of the spectrum, from red to violet. In 1668 he had used his research to design an improved telescope. At this time all telescopes used curved pieces of glass, called lenses, but these produced blurred images with colored edges. Newton's telescope, sketched here in his notebook, used a curved mirror to focus light, and it did not produce unwanted colors.

THE *PRINCIPIA*

This is the title page of Newton's most important book, the *Principia*. Newton was following in Galileo's footsteps by explaining the world mathematically. The first part of the *Principia* explains that three basic laws (p. 30) govern the way in which objects move. Newton then describes his theory of gravity, the force that pulls falling objects down. Using his laws, Newton shows that it is the force of gravity that keeps the planets moving in orbits around the sun (p. 32). Finally, Newton uses his laws to predict that the earth must be a slightly flattened sphere and that comets orbit the sun in elongated oval-shaped paths. These predictions were later shown to be true.

Winding handle to turn the orrery

PHILOSOPHIÆ NATURALIS Principia MATHEMATICA

Newton's Laws in action

Nᴇᴡᴛᴏɴ's ꜰɪʀsᴛ ʟᴀᴡ states that if an object is not being pushed or pulled by a force, it will either stay still or keep moving in a straight line at a steady speed. It might be obvious that a stationary object will not move until a force acts on it, but it is less obvious that a moving object can continue to move without the help of a force. The tendency of an object to remain moving in a straight line at constant speed or to remain stationary is called inertia. Newton's Second Law defines what happens when a force acts on an object – the object accelerates in the direction in which the force is acting. A force acting on a stationary object starts it moving. A force acting on a moving object will speed it up, slow it down, or change the direction in which it is moving. The Third Law states that if an object is pushed or pulled, it will push or pull to an equal extent in the opposite direction. For example, if a bulldozer pushes against a wall, the wall will exert an equal and opposite force on the bulldozer.

FREE FALL
Falling objects, such as parachutists when they jump from a plane, accelerate because they are pulled downward by a force – gravity. If the effects of air resistance are ignored, the speed at which a freely falling object travels will increase by 32 ft/sec (9.8 m/sec) for every second that it is falling. Known as g, this is the acceleration due to gravity. In practice, at a certain speed the upward force of air resistance equals the downward force of gravity and at this speed, called terminal velocity (p. 42), an object ceases to accelerate. From then on it will fall at a constant speed.

FARMYARD ACTION
All of Newton's Laws are illustrated by a horse pulling a cart. When the cart is stationary, the horse must strain to apply a force in order to move it. For the cart to move, the horse's force must overcome the inertia of the cart and the frictional forces (p. 38) that prevent the cart from moving. Once there is an overall forward pull, the cart will accelerate forward, obeying the Second Law. The horse can then relax, reducing its pull until it matches the frictional drag of the cart. There is then no overall force acting and the cart will move forward at a constant speed, as the First Law predicts. According to the Third Law, the force applied by the horse that acts upon the cart will at all times be matched by an equal and opposite force applied by the cart and acting upon the horse.

Load

Frictional force acts to prevent the wheel from turning

SIGNS OF THE SHAKING EARTH
This ancient Chinese earthquake detector relies upon the inertia of a central pendulum, attached to a system of levers, to cause a ball to fall from a dragon's jaws into the mouth of a waiting frog when the bowl is shaken.

INTO SPACE

The takeoff of a rocket illustrates several points about Newton's Laws. The rocket engine shows the Third Law in action; the force with which the hot gases are blasted from the combustion chamber produces a reaction force on the rocket. This force lifts and accelerates the rocket, as the Second Law leads us to expect. The exact formulation of the Second Law shows that the acceleration produced depends upon the mass of the rocket. The smaller the mass, the greater the acceleration. For this reason, the rate of acceleration increases as the rocket's fuel is burnt up.

UNDER PRESSURE

The straining face of a weightlifter shows that large forces can be involved even when nothing is moving. According to Newton's Third Law, the force with which the athlete lifts the weight produces an equal downward force on his arms. The weight of the bar is transmitted down through his legs, and presses downward on the floor. The floor presses upward with an equal force. The force pressing down must equal the upward force. If the floor pushed less strongly, then the athlete would fall through it. If it pushed more strongly, then he would fly into the air.

PULL AWAY

Rowers make use of Newton's Third Law. When pulling on an oar, a rower pushes water backward. The backward force on the water produces an equal and opposite force which moves the boat forward. An added advantage is gained because the oar is a lever (p. 16); a short pull by the rower produces a longer movement at the other end of the oar.

UNDERWATER JET

A squid propels itself through the water using jet propulsion. It squirts water backward in order to move forward. According to Newton's Third Law, the force of the expelled water is balanced by a force that propels the animal forward. Jet and rocket engines work in the same way.

Forces are transmitted in both directions through the shafts

The horse's muscles apply a forward force to accelerate the load

Gravity: the long-range force

THE FORCE THAT MAKES OBJECTS FALL to the ground is also the force that keeps the planets in their orbits around the sun. Isaac Newton was the first person to realize this. The ancient Greeks thought that objects fell because they were seeking their natural places, and that the planets were moved by invisible crystal spheres (p. 6). Even Johannes Kepler, who showed in 1609 that the planets moved in elliptical, or slightly oval-shaped, orbits, thought that they were being supported by an invisible framework. In 1687 Newton proved in his book *Principia* that the planets orbit around the sun because there is a long-range force – gravity – attracting them toward the sun. He was also able to show that the force of gravity between the sun and a planet depends on the distance between the two. A planet twice as far from the sun as another will experience only one-quarter of the force; if it is three times as far away, the force will be one-ninth, and so on. Newton also showed that the force of gravitational attraction between two objects depends on their masses. The greater the mass of the objects, the greater the force pulling them together.

COMETS
Isaac Newton showed that comets were objects in elongated elliptical orbits around the sun. Their paths were therefore predictable, like those of the planets. Edmond Halley, who paid for the publication of Newton's book *Principia*, used Newton's ideas to predict that a comet seen in 1531, 1607, and 1682 would return in 1758. When the comet appeared on schedule, it became known as Halley's comet.

THE SUN'S FAMILY
This early 19th-century orrery shows the planets of our solar system. The planetary orbits are shown as being circular although they are actually very slightly oval. Neptune, whose orbit lies outside the orbits of Saturn and Uranus, is not shown, as it was not discovered until 1846. Pluto, the outermost planet of our solar system, was not discovered until 1930.

Uranus

Earth

Sun

Mercury

Jupiter

THE MOMENT OF DISCOVERY
Newton is said to have realized the wider importance of gravity in 1666 when he saw an apple fall from a tree in his garden. In the words of one of his contemporaries, "It came into his thought that the power of gravity (which brought the apple from the tree to the ground) was not limited to a certain distance from the earth but that this power must extend much further than is usually thought. Why not as high as the moon, said he to himself, and if so that must influence her motion. Whereupon he fell a-calculating what would be the effect."

THE MOON AND THE APPLE
Newton calculated the force needed to keep the moon in a circular orbit around the earth, and compared this with the force that accelerated the apple downward. After allowing for the fact that the moon is much farther from the earth and has a greater mass, he found that the two forces were the same. The circular motion of the moon and the fall of the apple were the results of the same force – gravity.

Venus

THE UNIVERSE OF COPERNICUS

Polish astronomer Nicolaus Copernicus (1473-1543) put forward the idea that the planets orbit around the sun and not the earth. His vision of the solar system is shown in this print. In 1514 Copernicus outlined his ideas in a pamphlet and sent it to a few scholars, but he hesitated to publish more widely, fearing the anger of the Church. It is said that the first printed copy of his book, *On the Revolutions of the Celestial Spheres*, was brought to him on his deathbed.

JOHANNES KEPLER (1571-1630)

German mathematician and astronomer Johannes Kepler discovered the laws of planetary motion by studying the orbit of Mars. His studies led him to declare that the planets moved in slightly elongated elliptical orbits, and not in circles as Copernicus had supposed. Kepler also discovered that there was a relationship between the speed of a planet's movement and its distance from the sun, each planet moving fastest as it passes closest to the sun. Isaac Newton provided the theoretical explanation for Kepler's discoveries.

Drawing pencil

Winding handle to operate the device

Central ring

Mars

Ellipses drawn by the ellipsograph

Saturn

DRAWING AN ELLIPSE

The path of a planet orbiting the Sun is not a perfect circle, but an ellipse, an oval shape like the ones drawn by this piece of apparatus. The device is called an ellipsograph and it was made in 1817 by John Farey of London. An ellipse is a combination of two circular motions. The drawing pencil is fixed in position in the central ring, which then revolves. At the same time, the ring itself is carried round in a circle and the pencil traces the combination of these two paths. The simplest way to draw an ellipse is by tying the ends of a piece of thin string to two tacks and then sticking the tacks into a sheet of cardboard so that the string is loose. When a pencil is placed against the string so that it pulls the string tight, the path that the pencil will trace as it moves around is an ellipse. An ellipse has two focuses – the tacks in this case. The orbit of a planet has the sun as one of the focuses of the ellipse around which it travels. Each planet travels fastest when it is closest to the sun and slowest when it is furthest away.

PULLING THE WATER

The rise and fall of the tides is caused by gravity. The oceans on the side of the earth nearest to the moon are pulled outward by the force of the moon's gravity, creating a high tide. At the same time a high tide occurs on the opposite side of the earth because the moon's gravity is less there and the water bulges away. The sun has a smaller effect on the planet's water, but when the moon and the sun are in line, at the new or full moon, their forces combine to produce extremely high and low "spring" tides. When they are at right angles, less extreme "neap" tides occur.

Weight and mass

An astronaut standing on the moon weighs only one-sixth as much as on earth. This is because the weight of an object is due to the downward force of gravity acting upon it. The force of gravity on the surface of a planet depends upon the mass of the planet and its size. Gravity on the surface of the moon is only one-sixth as strong as gravity on earth. Jupiter's surface gravity is 2.64 times that of the earth, so an object would weigh 2.64 times as much there. An object's mass, on the other hand, is the amount of material that it contains, and this remains constant. Mass is a measure of an object's resistance to being accelerated by a force. The same force would be needed to roll a bowling ball on Jupiter as is needed on Earth.

MEASURING MASS
A balance, like this Roman steelyard from Pompeii, really measures mass rather than weight. Since the force of gravity is the same at both ends of the beam, which acts as a lever, the measurement that it gives would be the same here or on the moon. It does not depend upon gravity. The small mass (confusingly called a "weight") is moved to the left until it balances with the object whose mass is being measured. This mass is shown by the scale along the beam.

Fulcrum

Beam with scale

Weight

TWO-PAN BALANCE
This money changer's balance, made in 1653, was used for valuing coins of pure gold. A coin of unknown value is placed in one pan, and its value in other currencies can be found by balancing it against fixed weights from the box below, which represent coins from other countries.

Unknown coin

Standard weight

SCALES OF JUSTICE
The balance has been used since ancient times. This scene from an Egyptian papyrus shows the jackal-headed god, Anubis (left) weighing the heart of Princess Nesitanebtashru (right) on the Day of Judgment. Her heart, in an urn on the right-hand pan, is being balanced against the goddess of truth and righteousness on the left-hand pan.

Scale pan

Grapes whose mass is being measured

LOCAL STANDARDS
The need to weigh precious metals accurately has led people in many countries to develop their own systems of fixed, or standard, weights. On the right are some examples of weights from around the world.

Assyrian lion

Dial showing
weight in
pounds

Needle

110 0
100
90
80
70
60
50
40
30
20
10

7 lb (3.2 kg) weight

Oval spring

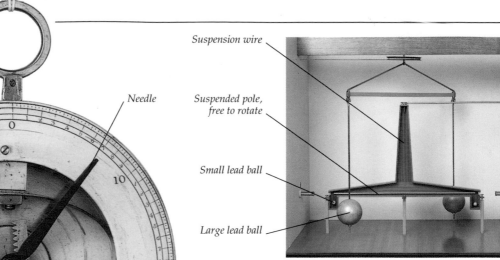

Suspension wire

*Suspended pole,
free to rotate*

Small lead ball

Large lead ball

THE MASS OF THE EARTH

In 1798 English scientist Henry Cavendish used this apparatus, which filled a whole room, to calculate the mass of the earth. Two small lead balls hang from the ends of a pole that is suspended from a wire and free to revolve. A beam supporting two large balls is turned so that the large and small balls approach each other. The gravitational attraction between the large and the small balls causes the pole to revolve, and by measuring this deflection Cavendish was able to calculate the gravitational attraction between balls of known masses at a given distance apart. Using Newton's Law of Gravity (p. 32), he was then able to calculate the mass that the earth must have in order to produce the gravitational force observed at its surface. His result? The mass of the Earth is 6 million, million, million, million kilograms.

MEASURING WEIGHT

A spring balance, like this 18th-century example, really does measure weight. The oval spring stretches when a weight is hung from the balance, turning a needle and giving a reading on the dial. This reading varies with gravity. On the moon, for example, the spring balance would indicate a weight one-sixth of that shown here. Weight is in fact a force, and its correct metric unit is the newton, named after the great scientist (p. 30). This is appropriate since one newton is about the weight of a large apple. However, it is more common to use the kilogram weight, the weight of one kilogram mass in earth's gravity, as the metric unit of weight.

TOPPLING OVER

Every object has a "center of gravity," through which the force of gravity seems to act. An object is stable if this center of gravity is directly over its base. In the case of this hay cart, the base is a line between the two wheels. If the cart is tilted further, so that a line drawn down from its center of gravity falls outside the wheel, it will become unstable and topple over.

BALANCING ACT

In order to remain balanced, the center of gravity of a pyramid of acrobats must be precisely above the feet of the lowest person. If the pyramid starts to topple, the acrobats must lean away from the fall, moving their center of gravity back to the stable position.

STANDARD KILOGRAM

Travel and trade require worldwide units with commonly agreed values. The Standard International metric unit of mass is the kilogram, like the one below. Mass and volume are connected, because one liter of pure water weighs precisely 1 kg (2.2 lb).

Chinese jade

Siamese dragon

Ashanti warrior

Burmese elephant

Standard kilogram

Collisions

IMAGINE A TRUCK SPEEDING ALONG A ROAD. A car pulls out in front of the truck, and a collision looks likely. The driver applies the brakes but only just manages to slow the truck down in time. This is because the momentum of the truck carries it forward. The greater the speed of the truck, the more momentum it has and the harder it is to stop quickly. Furthermore, the heavier the truck's load, the harder it is to stop. The momentum of any moving object depends on both its speed and its mass. The effects of a collision can often be predicted by calculating the momentum of the objects involved, owing to the fact that when objects collide, their total momentum is unchanged by the collision, provided that no other forces are acting. This is called the Law of Conservation of Momentum, and it applies to all moving objects. Unless other forces act, the momentum of the truck will not change. In practice, frictional forces (p. 38) tend to reduce an object's momentum. The brakes that slow the truck down work in this way.

HOT METAL
The blacksmith's anvil is so massive that it is hardly moved by the blows from the hammer. Instead, the momentum of the hammer is absorbed by the hot metal of the horseshoe, which is beaten into shape.

Incoming white ball collides with first red ball

Momentum passes through the red balls, which remain stationary

CONSERVATION OF MOMENTUM
The total momentum of colliding objects is the same before and after the collision. In the picture above, a white billiard ball collides from the left with a row of stationary red balls, and stops dead at the left-hand end of the row. A single yellow ball moves away from the right-hand end of the row. The momentum of the white ball has passed, unchanged, right through the row of reds and into the yellow ball. Since the yellow ball has exactly the same mass as the white, it accelerates to exactly the same speed that the white ball was traveling before the collision. If the yellow had twice the mass of the white, it would move away at half the speed.

AT AN ANGLE (*left*)
Momentum has a direction, as well as a size. If two billiard balls collide off-center, they rebound at an angle. However, the total momentum is still the same before and after the collision. Before the collision the momentum was carried by the single white ball moving directly toward the stationary yellow ball at a certain speed. After the collision the momentum is shared between the white ball and the yellow ball, and both balls now move more slowly than the original speed. Although neither ball is now moving directly to the right, each ball has some momentum towards the right and the total rightward momentum remains the same as before the collision.

A DESTRUCTIVE COLLISION

A heavy steel ball being swung on a chain has considerable momentum. When the ball strikes the wall, this momentum is transferred. The wall starts to move, the cement between the bricks is torn apart and the bricks themselves, because they are light, are knocked away.

METEORITE CRATER

The effects of a meteor colliding with the earth are seen at the Barringer crater, a circular depression about 4,000 ft (1,200 m) across, near Winslow, Arizona. The wall surrounding the crater rises 160 ft (50 m) above the plain. Attempts have been made to find the remains of a large meteorite under the soil, but only small pieces have been found. Large meteorites generally disintegrate when they hit the earth.

TAKING THE STRAIN

Taken at the moment of impact, this photograph shows one side of a golf ball being flattened by the face of the colliding golf club. This illustrates the great forces generated by the swinging club. Because the ball distorts rather than moving away immediately, the club stays in contact with the ball for longer and more power can be transferred to the ball. The club is far heavier than the ball, and, because total momentum is conserved, the ball will move faster after the collision than the club moved before the collision.

Momentum is passed to yellow ball, which accelerates away

BIG GUNS

A British gun in action during World War I recoils as a shell is fired. This is a consequence of Newton's Third Law (p. 30); the force propelling the shell forward is matched by an equal and opposite reaction force which drives the gun backward. The momentum of a recoiling gun is equal and opposite to the momentum of the shell, producing a total momentum of zero – the same as before firing. Since the mass of the gun is so much larger than the mass of the shell, the shell moves forward with a far greater speed than the gun moves back.

SUBATOMIC COLLISIONS

In this photograph of a collision between subatomic particles in a bubble chamber, a kaon particle (yellow) has entered at the bottom and collided with a proton to produce pions (orange and mauve tracks). An invisible lambda particle is also created, and its mass can be calculated using the laws that describe the collisions of particles.

Friction

RIDING HIGH
No one could ride a bike, or even walk, without friction. It is the friction between the tires and the ground that prevents the bike from slipping down the slope.

GALILEO AND NEWTON realized that everyday experience makes it difficult to understand force and motion. People are used to seeing moving objects slow down and stop when the force pushing them is removed. Galileo and Newton said that this is because there is usually a force – called friction – acting to slow moving objects. Remove friction, they said, and moving objects would continue to move without being pushed. For instance, a stone skidding across a frozen pond travels an enormous distance because there is little friction between the stone and the icy lake surface. (This is because a thin layer of water keeps the stone and the ice apart.) Friction is the force that opposes the movement of objects sliding over each other. Friction occurs because no surface is perfectly smooth, however flat it may appear. All surfaces consist of tiny "hills and valleys," and where the microscopic peaks on the two surfaces come in contact they can weld together, making it difficult for one surface to slide over the other. Friction increases as the pressure between the two surfaces increases. The heavier an object, the greater the number of peaks that come in contact and the greater the number of tiny welds. This makes heavier objects harder to slide.

ELECTRICITY BY FRICTION
Early electrical machines produced electricity by rubbing a rotating glass plate with a leather or silk pad. Francis Hauksbee, maker of scientific apparatus and unofficial Curator of Experiments at the Royal Society in London, made one of the first frictional electrical machines in about 1710. This machine has four fixed pads that press against a circular glass plate. When the plate is spun, an electrical charge is created. This charge is carried away by four wire-tipped arms, and it builds up on the surface of the tube. The electricity can be discharged at a chosen voltage by adjusting the gap across which it must spark.

Friction pad

Glass plate

Mouthpiece

Tube to store charge

Adjusting knob to regulate voltage

Wire-tipped arm

Handle to rotate glass plate

Firestick

Leather thong

Point at which friction creates heat

Wooden firestick made and used by the Inuit people of the Arctic

HEAT FROM FRICTION
Rubbing two sticks together is a very ancient way of making fire. The Inuit firestick is more sophisticated: a leather thong is wound around the upright stick, and when this is pulled back and forth the stick spins at high speed. The end of the stick becomes hot and ignites the tinder. In the same way, when a match is struck, friction causes the chemicals in the match head to ignite. Friction also heats up the pads and discs in a car's braking system and causes the Space Shuttle to heat up as it reenters the earth's atmosphere from space.

HOUSE OF CARDS

Without friction, a house of cards would collapse. Friction between the cards keeps them in place so long as they are at a steep angle. The same is true of a ladder. The angle at which the cards or the ladder will begin to slip is determined by the "limiting friction," or the maximum friction that can occur between the touching surfaces. In 1781 the French physicist Charles de Coulomb found that the limiting friction did not depend upon the area in contact, only on the materials involved and the pressure between the surfaces. Coulomb introduced the term "coefficient of friction" to describe a value that indicates the frictional force of a particular surface under standard conditions. Slippery substances have a low coefficient of friction.

UNDER THE MICROSCOPE

This is the surface of a piece of paper, magnified 100 times by a powerful microscope. Although the paper looks smooth to the naked eye, the microscope reveals the small-scale roughness that causes friction. When one surface is pressing against another, the pressure on the points of contact can be immense, creating bonds between the surfaces. Friction, a resistance to motion, is caused by these bonds.

FLOATING ON AIR

This is the first hovercraft ever built, making its first public appearance in 1959. The hovercraft was invented by British engineer Christopher Cockerell. In 1955, in an attempt to design a boat that would slide over water as easily as a skate slides over ice, Cockerell thought of using a cushion of air under pressure to hold the boat away from the water and so reduce friction. His idea proved so successful that hovercraft are now used in many parts of the world for crossing calm waters at high speed.

Ball bearings in a race *Oil*

Ball bearing

ROLLING AND SLIDING

Ball bearings reduce friction by rolling rather than dragging across a surface, in the same way that a wheel reduces the friction of a load being moved over a surface (p. 11). When held in a cage, or race, ball bearings allow a wheel to turn freely on an axle passing through the inner ring. Lubricants such as oil and grease are also used in machines to reduce friction. They form a thin layer between moving surfaces, preventing them from rubbing together.

STREAMLINING

An object moving through a liquid or gas also experiences friction which causes drag, slowing the object down. To reduce this drag, ships, submarines, racing cars, and aircraft are all streamlined – shaped so that water or air will flow smoothly over their surfaces when they are moving at speed. Such craft are often tapered to a point at the back. Dolphins, fish, and sharks are well streamlined and glide through water with ease.

Energy

WHEN ISAAC NEWTON FORMULATED his Laws of Motion (p. 30) in 1687, he did not mention energy. English scientist Thomas Young first used the word, in its scientific sense, 80 years after the death of Newton. According to Young, a moving object has energy because it can be made to do work – anything that can do work has energy. A moving object could, for example, drag a small cart along. Today we call the energy of a moving object "kinetic energy." Scottish engineer William Rankine coined the term "potential energy," half a century after Young, to describe the energy possessed by a raised weight. A raised weight can do work; if allowed to fall down, the weight can hammer a pile into the ground. In 1847 English scientist James Joule showed that heat was a form of energy, too. The steam engine, invented by English engineer Thomas Newcomen in 1712, was a device for using heat to do work. Joule discovered that the amount of potential or kinetic energy needed to produce a unit of heat was always the same. This discovery led to the Law of Conservation of Energy, one of the most important laws in science.

ENERGY PIONEER
James Prescott Joule (1818-1889) was born in Salford, England. Joule studied the heating effect of an electric current and realized that heat was energy. A unit of energy was named after him.

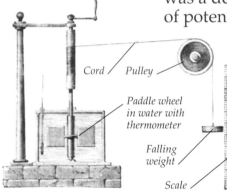

Cord / Pulley

Paddle wheel in water with thermometer

Falling weight

Scale

JOULE'S EXPERIMENT
This apparatus was used by James Joule to measure the mechanical equivalent of heat. The falling weight turned a paddle wheel in a container of water, and the water became slightly warmer. Joule then compared the work done by the falling weight with the heat produced. By using different weights and letting them fall different heights, Joule found that the same amount of work always produced the same amount of heat.

ENERGY QUALITY
This is a model of a fairground steam engine built in 1934 by John Fowler of Leeds, England, to run an electricity generator. Electricity is a high-quality form of energy. It can easily be converted into other forms of energy, so it is very versatile. Low-quality energy, such as sound or waste heat, cannot easily be changed into other forms and is less useful. Whenever energy is transformed the amount of low-quality energy always increases, though the total amount of energy remains constant. Steam engines, for instance, always produce useless waste heat. This is why a perpetual motion machine cannot be built – such machines always lose useful energy in the form of waste heat, principally because of friction.

ENERGY TRANSFORMATIONS
Energy can take many different forms – kinetic, potential, electrical, heat, sound, light, chemical – and they are all interchangeable. Chemical energy can be changed into heat by burning a fuel. Heat can produce kinetic energy in an engine. Kinetic energy can be changed into electrical energy by a generator. An electric bulb produces light. An electric range produces heat. A radio emits sound energy and a fan converts electrical energy to kinetic energy. During these transformations the total amount of energy after the change is the same as the amount before the change. Energy cannot be destroyed or created. This is called the Law of Conservation of Energy.

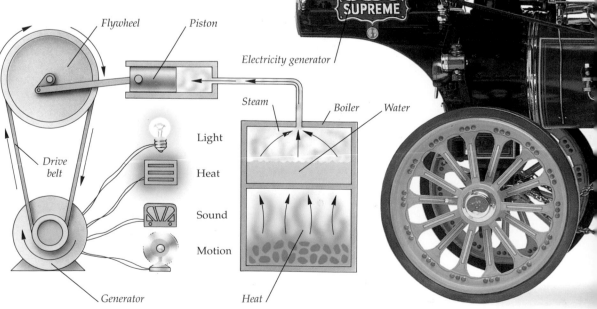

Flywheel   Piston

Electricity generator

Steam   Boiler   Water

Light

Drive belt

Heat

Sound

Motion

Generator

Heat

A. DEAKIN & S

SUPREME

ROLLER COASTER

As a roller coaster car rushes up and down, its energy changes from kinetic to potential and back again. Kinetic energy is greatest when the car is going at its greatest speed. The car has maximum potential energy when it is at its highest point.

THE WIND OF CHANGE

This wind farm near Palm Springs, California, converts the kinetic energy of the wind into electrical energy. Wind and waves are created by the heat of the sun – their energy is a form of solar energy. The rate at which energy reaches the earth in the form of sunlight is more than 12,000 times greater than the rate at which humans consume fuel. Although solar energy is spread out and difficult to collect, it can provide a clean, safe, and renewable source of energy to replace the use of fossil fuels and nuclear power.

ENGINE POWER

The energy held in fuels such as gasoline is called chemical energy. Engines such as this twin-cylinder aircraft engine convert the chemical energy to kinetic energy, plus waste heat and sound. The power of an engine is a measure of the energy it converts in a given time. A high-power engine is one that can convert energy quickly. A unit used to measure power is the watt (or joule per second), named after Scottish engineer James Watt (p. 21), who produced the first efficient steam engine in 1776.

Spark plug

Carburetor

Cylinder head

Propeller

Flywheel

S. MODERN AMUSEMENTS

Drive belt

LIGHT AND SOUND

The busy fairground is an energy-packed place. Electricity, the most versatile form of energy, drives almost all of the machines, being converted into motion and heat, bright lights and music. The people, too, are driven by energy – chemical energy from their food.

Combined forces

MOST OBJECTS HAVE MORE THAN one force acting on them. For instance, a yacht sailing across the sea has the force of the wind on its sails. Resistance forces of the air and water act to slow down any motion. In addition, the weight of the yacht pulls down, while the buoyancy force of the water lifts the boat. There is also a force produced by the heavy keel of the yacht that prevents it from tipping. The combined effect of all these forces is called the resultant – the single force that has the same effect as many forces acting on an object. In many situations the forces cancel each other out and the resultant is zero, meaning that no overall force is acting and that the object is moving at a constant speed or it is stationary. An object whose speed is not changing is said to be in a state of equilibrium.

AIR FORCE
Fighter aircraft are acted on by several forces. Gravity pulls them downward; the wings provide a lifting force; air resistance produces a drag, or slowing, force; and the engine provides a forward thrust. The pilot must balance the aircraft's weight, thrust, lift, and drag to produce the correct overall resultant force in the required direction.

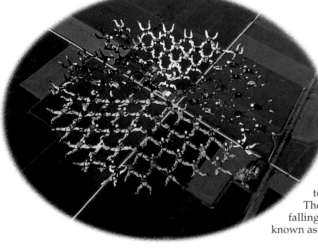

HIGH-SPEED EQUILIBRIUM
These skydivers are in equilibrium because they are being acted upon by two equal and opposite forces. The force of gravity accelerating them downward is exactly matched by the force of their air resistance, which acts to slow them down. They are therefore falling at a constant speed, known as terminal velocity.

ON THE HIGH SEAS
A yacht can sail in many directions, and not only in the direction that the wind is blowing. This versatility is achieved by moving the sail around to catch the force of the wind at different angles. The force of the wind acting on the sails is transferred to the yacht through the mast. Some of this force will be in directions other than forward, and the keel helps to counteract the sideways component of this force. The pressure of the water against the keel prevents the yacht from moving sideways. To find the resultant of these two forces, or any other pair of forces, geometry is needed, because the effect of a force depends upon its direction as well as its size. If two forces acting on an object are represented by the sides of a parallelogram (with the angle between them representing their relative directions and the lengths of the lines representing the sizes of the two forces) then the resultant force acting on the object is represented by the diagonal of the parallelogram (below). This useful diagram is called the parallelogram of forces.

Parallelogram of forces

Force on yacht from the effect of wind on the sails

Force on yacht from the effect of water against the keel

Resultant force on yacht

Pressure of water against the keel produces a sideways force on the yacht, preventing it from slipping sideways

THE SCIENCE OF STATICS
The science of statics studies the forces acting on objects that are at rest. The earliest investigation into statics was made by Archimedes in ancient Greece. Architects use statics to understand the forces acting on buildings. The weight of the roof and upper walls of this cathedral is enormous, and the lower walls must be thick to bear the load. Flying buttresses support the walls and spread the load.

BRIDGE BUILDING
Bridge builders use statics to calculate the loads that will be supported by the bridge. The forces tending to bend the bridge and make it collapse must never exceed the forces tending to keep the bridge straight. In a suspension bridge the load is borne by flexible cables, which are in turn supported by towers at each end. These towers are built to withstand extremely strong forces. Since this kind of bridge can tend to sway in strong winds, the road is often stiffened with a beam or a girder shaped like a hollow box.

PRESSING DOWN
In this human pyramid, the weight of each person is spread to the two people below who are linked to each other, thus forming a stack of triangles.

Wind acts on the sails to produce a force

THE STRONG TRIANGLE
The triangle is often used in buildings, bridges, and towers because of its strong rigid shape. A structure made of beams connected together in triangles cannot be twisted or collapsed without deforming the beams. The triangle is the only geometric shape with this property. The 984-ft (300-m) Eiffel Tower in Paris, built in 1889, is made almost entirely of triangles. The wide base supports almost 8,000 tons of iron and steel.

THE BUCKYBALL
This newly found carbon molecule is now known as buckminsterfullerene because its molecules resemble the geodesic domes designed by the American inventor, Buckminster Fuller. The molecules, nicknamed buckyballs, each consist of 60 carbon atoms forming pentagons and hexagons (5- and 6-sided figures). Each atom is held in place by the combined forces from its neighboring atoms, producing a very stable structure.

The weight of the yacht acts downward on the water

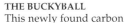

Pressure of water on the rudder produces a force to turn the yacht

Upthrust due to weight of displaced water acts upwards on the yacht

Pressure and flow

IF TWO PEOPLE OF THE SAME WEIGHT walk on deep snow, one wearing ordinary shoes and one wearing snowshoes, the person wearing the ordinary shoes will sink deeper than the other. In both cases the weight on the snow is the same, but the snowshoes spread the weight over a larger area. The force under a snowshoe is less concentrated than that under an ordinary shoe. This shows the importance of pressure, or force per unit area. In many situations it is pressure rather than force that matters. A thumbtack has a large head to spread the force of the thumb, but a sharp point to concentrate the force on to a tiny area, producing great pressure. A sharp knife cuts well because the force of the cut is concentrated into the small area of the cutting edge. Liquids and gases exert pressure; any object that is put in a liquid has pressure on its sides. The pressure is caused by the weight of the fluid above it.

POND WALKER
A bird walks across the delicate leaf of a water plant. The bird's long toes are splayed to spread its weight, reducing the pressure on the leaf. This prevents the bird from sinking or breaking through the leaf.

THE MAGDEBURG SPHERES
In 1654 Otto von Guericke, mayor of the German town of Magdeburg, performed a spectacular demonstration of the air's pressure. He made two round cups of copper that fitted together to form a hollow ball. When the air inside the ball was pumped out, the air pressing on the outside held the two cups together so firmly that it was impossible to pull them apart, even by hanging heavy weights from the lower cup. When the air was allowed back into the ball, returning the inside pressure to normal, the two cups simply fell apart.

MEASURING AIR PRESSURE
Air pressure is measured by using a barometer. The mercury barometer, like this example, was invented in 1643 by Galileo's pupil Evangelista Torricelli (1608-1647). A tube, sealed at one end, is filled with mercury and then turned upside down in a small bulb of mercury. The mercury in the tube falls until its weight is supported by the pressure of the air on the surface of the mercury in the bulb. Air pressure can therefore be determined by measuring the height of the column of mercury. Mercury is used because it is extremely dense and the supported column is of a manageable height.

BLAISE PASCAL (1623-1662)
Frenchman Blaise Pascal packed three careers into his short life: scientist, mathematician, and religious thinker. When he was 19 years old he made the first successful calculating machine to help his father with his business accounts. In 1646 he made a mercury barometer and later demonstrated that it measured air pressure, by showing that the mercury level fell as the barometer was carried up a mountain. He concentrated on mathematics after an intense religious experience in 1654. A unit of pressure, the pascal, is named after him.

UNDER THE SEA
The pressure in any liquid depends on the liquid's depth; the greater the depth, the greater the pressure. A diver in deep water must be able to survive great pressures, so diving helmets are thick and strong. Pressure also depends on the density of the liquid; mercury exerts more pressure than a less dense liquid such as water.

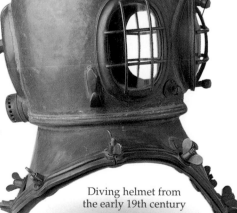

Air supply

Window of strengthened glass

Diving helmet from the early 19th century

Small weight

Large weight

Liquid

PASCAL'S PRINCIPLE
Pascal's Principle states that in a liquid or gas at rest, the pressure is transmitted equally in all directions. Many kinds of hydraulic devices, such as the car jack, work on this principle. As this engraving shows, a small weight pressing on a narrow column of liquid is able to support a large weight on a wide column connected to it. The pressure in both columns is the same, but as the large column has a greater area it produces a larger total force.

TEST FLIGHT
This model plane is used in a wind tunnel to study the way that air flows over the wings of a real plane. As air moves over the plane's surfaces, the speed of the air changes and this can alter its pressure.

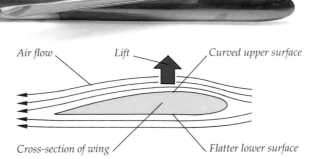

BERNOULLI'S PRINCIPLE
In a moving fluid – a liquid or a gas – the pressure decreases as the speed of flow increases. This is called Bernoulli's principle, and it explains why an aircraft wing produces lift. Air flowing over the curved top of the wing must travel farther than air passing under the wing, and it therefore moves more swiftly, producing an area of low pressure above the wing. The greater pressure under the wing causes the wing to rise.

Air flow — *Lift* — *Curved upper surface*

Cross-section of wing — *Flatter lower surface*

DANIEL BERNOULLI (1700-1782)
Daniel Bernoulli of Switzerland came from a family of brilliant mathematicians. His uncle Jakob discovered a series of complex fractions that are used in higher mathematics and are now known as Bernoulli numbers. His father Johann concentrated on applied mathematics. Daniel made important discoveries in trigonometry and wrote a book on hydrodynamics, the study of moving fluids.

Knobs to adjust flow of air and paint

Air supply tube

Nozzle

230

Trigger

Paint supply tube

BERNOULLI'S PRINCIPLE IN ACTION
The heart of a spray gun consists of two fine tubes. One leads up from a reservoir of paint and the other directs a flow of high-speed air across the top of the paint tube. In accordance with Bernoulli's principle, the fast flow of air creates low pressure above the paint tube, sucking paint upwards into the air stream. The paint is broken into droplets and carried to the target.

Cutaway of air supply tube

Reduced pressure

Cutaway of paint supply tube

Paint is drawn up the tube and broken into tiny droplets

Compressed air supply

Paint reservoir

PRESSURE AT WORK
The spray gun was invented by Doctor De Vilbiss of Toledo, Ohio, in the early 1800s. He used it to blow medicine down infected throats. After a time the spray gun became more widely used, mainly for applying coatings such as paints, lacquers, and glazes. The gun relies on high pressure or compressed air for its power. The compressed air enters the gun from an inlet in the handle and passes through a valve controlled by a trigger. The air then travels through the gun to the paint nozzle, where it draws the paint out of its container by suction. The paint is atomized – broken up into tiny droplets – by the air stream, and a fine mist of paint spray is blown forward on to the surface being painted. The airbrush, used in artwork and graphic design, operates on exactly the same principle.

Back and forth

Wₕₑₙ ₐ ₜₑᵢ𝓰ₕₜ is HUNG FROM A SPRING and given a slight downward push, it will dance up and down. Movements like this, in which an object moves repeatedly back and forth, are called oscillations or vibrations. When a weight is hung from a string and pushed to one side, it will swing from side to side in a regular way. This, too, is an oscillation, and this simple device – called a pendulum – provides a method of timekeeping because its oscillations are very regular. The number of times that a particular pendulum swings each second – called its frequency – is always the same, provided the swing is small. Legend has it that Galileo noticed this one morning while sitting in church. During a boring sermon, his attention turned to a lamp that was swinging from the ceiling at the end of a long rope. The lamp seemed to be taking the same time to make each swing, but like all good scientists Galileo needed exact data. He timed the swings using his own pulse as a clock, an experiment that could be conducted without attracting attention. He was able to confirm his initial impression and later designed a clock which made use of a pendulum (p. 25).

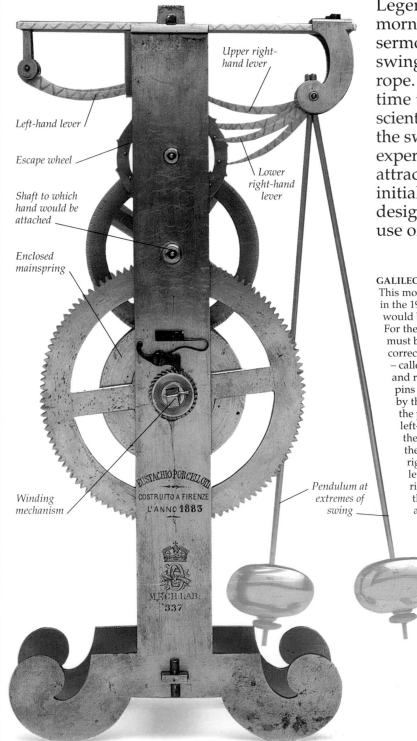

Left-hand lever

Escape wheel

Shaft to which hand would be attached

Enclosed mainspring

Upper right-hand lever

Lower right-hand lever

EUSTACHIO PORCELLOTTI

COSTRUITO A FIRENZE

L'ANNO 1883

M.ECH.LAB. 337

Winding mechanism

Pendulum at extremes of swing

GALILEO'S CLOCK – A DOUBLE EXPOSURE
This model of Galileo's clock was made in Italy in the 19th century. A shaft, to which a hand would be attached, is driven by a large spring. For the clock to work, the power of this spring must be released slowly and at exactly the correct rate. To achieve this, the top gear wheel – called the escape wheel – is regularly held and released by levers that fit into teeth and pins on the wheel. The levers are operated by the regular swing of the pendulum. As the pendulum swings outward, the left-hand lever drops down, stopping the escape wheel from turning. When the pendulum swings in, the upper right-hand lever lifts the left-hand lever, releasing the wheel. The lower right-hand lever is pushed down by the pins on the escape wheel as it turns, and this keeps the pendulum swinging.

A side view of Galileo's clock

BEATING TIME
A metronome is a device used to help musicians keep a regular pace or beat. The beat is adjusted by moving a weight up or down the swinging arm. This changes the effective length of the pendulum and therefore its frequency.

Christian Huygens
(1629-1695)

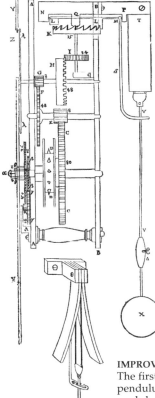

MEASURING GRAVITY

This piece of equipment, packed with all its accessories in a strong box for safe transport, is called an invariable pendulum. At one end of the pendulum is a knife-edged pivot on which it swings, and at the other end is a heavy weight.

The rate at which a pendulum swings changes with its length and with the force of gravity. Since this "invariable" pendulum has a fixed length, its rate of swing can be used to determine the force of gravity at different places around the globe. Gravity decreases with the distance from the center of the earth, so the pendulum can be used to determine the shape of the planet, which is slightly flattened at the North and South Poles.

Between 1828 and 1840 this particular pendulum was taken to the South Atlantic, the Euphrates River in Iraq, and Antarctica.

Knife-edged pivot

THE SPINNING EARTH

Léon Foucault is best known for using a pendulum to demonstrate the rotation of the earth. In 1851 he suspended a very large iron ball by a long steel wire from the center of the dome of the Pantheon in Paris. When the pendulum was first released it swung along a line marked on the floor beneath it, but after several hours the pendulum appeared to have changed direction. In fact, Foucault's pendulum was still swinging in the same direction – it was the earth below the pendulum that had turned.

Léon Foucault
(1819-1868)

Fixed heavy weight

IMPROVED ACCURACY

The first practical pendulum clock was made by Dutch scientist Christian Huygens in 1657. These drawings are taken from his book *Horologium Oscillatorium* of 1673. His design used a short pendulum and a weight to drive the hands. An endless chain or rope provided the drive, even when the clock was being wound. This arrangement is still used today in "grandfather" clocks. The lower drawing shows the curved, or "cycloidal," cheeks between which the pendulum swung for greater accuracy.

THE BALANCE SPRING

In 1675 Huygens made a watch regulated by an oscillating spring, called a balance spring or hairspring. Many clocks and watches have since used this mechanism. This model shows how the mechanism works. One end of the hairspring is fixed and the other end is attached to the center of the balance wheel. The spring alternately winds and unwinds, spinning the wheel back and forth. The rate of the oscillations can be adjusted by altering the tension in the spring, or by turning the cylindrical screws around the balance wheel.

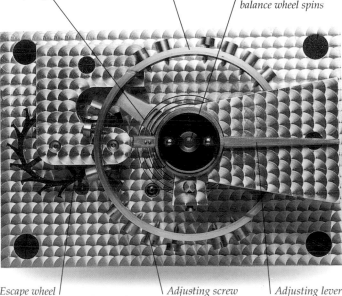

Hairspring *Balance wheel* *Ruby bearing on which balance wheel spins*

Escape wheel *Adjusting screw* *Adjusting lever*

Giant vibrations

SOLDIERS NEVER MARCH IN STEP across a bridge. This is because any bridge will vibrate slightly as the soldiers cross, and if the rhythm of the vibrations matches the rhythm of the soldier's steps, the marching could shake the bridge to pieces. Anything that can vibrate – a swing, a pendulum, or a tuning fork – has its own natural rhythm, or natural frequency. This is the number of vibrations that the object makes each second when it vibrates. If an object is given a single push, it will start to vibrate at its natural frequency, but the vibrations will die down unless it is given regular pushes or pulls. A child's swing will gradually stop swinging if left alone, but if it is pushed with the correct rhythm it can be made to rise higher and higher. This happens when the frequency of the pushes is the same as the natural frequency of the swing. Increasing the size – or amplitude – of a vibration by regular pushes is called resonance. A bridge will resonate and may even be destroyed if the rhythm of the marching soldiers' steps is the same as the natural frequency of the bridge.

HIGHER AND HIGHER
For a swing to go high, it must be pushed at the beginning of each swing. The frequency of the pushes must match the natural frequency of the swing. Pushing with any other rhythm will slow the swing down.

MUSICAL RESONANCE
The sound box of a violin or other stringed musical instrument increases the sound of each vibrating string by resonance. Bowing the string causes it to vibrate, producing a sound. These vibrations start the bridge vibrating, and this in turn spreads the vibrations to the whole body, since the front and back are connected by a post. This amplifies the sound. The violin is built so that its sound box resonates to a wide range of notes, amplifying them all equally.

WIND INSTRUMENTS
In woodwind instruments, such as the Pan pipes (above) and the fife (right), a column of air vibrates in a tube. The air in each tube of the Pan pipes vibrates strongly at only one fundamental frequency, which depends on the length of the tube; the longer the tube, the lower the resonant frequency. In the fife, the frequency of the vibration is altered by covering holes to change the effective length of the tube.

VIBRATING STRINGS
The simplest way that a stretched string can vibrate is shown below. The middle of the string moves strongly back and forth. This point of maximum movement is called an antinode. The points of minimum movements, called nodes, are at the ends of the string. This vibration produces a note called the fundamental. However, strings can also vibrate in more complicated ways. The other vibrations are called harmonics. The first harmonic occurs when a string vibrates in two halves, with a node at its center. The frequency of this vibration is twice that of the fundamental. Other harmonics occur when the string vibrates in three, four, or more sections. Strings, therefore, resonate with more than one frequency, although the fundamental frequency is always the strongest. Vibrating columns of air, which are created in the tubes of instruments such as flutes and organs, show the same behavior, producing a fundamental note and a series of harmonics.

Vibrating string

BAFFLING THE ECHOES

Concert halls are designed to suppress unwanted resonances. In a badly designed hall, sound waves of certain frequencies can be repeatedly reflected back and forth between the walls and the ceiling, producing an amplification of certain musical notes. Particular notes might sound quiet in some parts of the hall and very loud in others. In this hall, geometrical shapes called "baffles" have been hung from the ceiling to absorb unwanted echoes.

NUCLEAR RESONANCE

The technique of nuclear magnetic resonance (NMR) uses the fact that the nuclei of some atoms behave like small magnets. In an oscillating magnetic field, these nuclear magnets vibrate back and forth, and since the frequency at which a nucleus absorbs the maximum energy is its natural frequency, NMR can be used to identify the composition of chemical compounds (above). NMR can also be used in a scanner as an alternative to X-rays. By passing a radio wave over a patient's body and noting where energy is absorbed by resonance between the waves and the nuclei in the body, a computer can create a picture of the patient's internal organs.

EXPLODING WINEGLASS

Resonance occurs because energy is transferred to the vibrating object, building up and increasing the amplitude, or size, of the vibration. In some situations, the energy transferred can be destructive. A wineglass can be exploded by a sound wave if the frequency of the sound wave matches the natural frequency of the glass. The natural vibrations of a wineglass are of high frequency or pitch. This can be demonstrated by running a wet finger rapidly around the rim of the glass, producing a ringing note. If a singer now sings this note loudly, the glass resonates with the sound. The size of these vibrations can be enough to break the glass apart. This transfer of energy during resonance plays an important part in the tuning of a radio or a television. In both cases the tuning circuit consists of components in which electric current flows back and forth. The frequency at which the current oscillates can be varied to match the frequency of the signal being received by the aerial. This sets up resonance in the circuit, enabling it to absorb the maximum energy from the aerial signal, and this produces the clearest picture or sound.

TACOMA NARROWS COLLAPSE

During a storm in November 1940, the bridge over the Tacoma Narrows in Washington State began to twist back and forth so violently that it finally collapsed, only four months after it was opened. The very strong wind just happened to set up a twisting motion at the natural frequency of the 2,800-ft (860-m) bridge.

Antinode

Node

Making waves

ENERGY IS NOT ONLY continually changing form – it is also continually moving from one place to another. One way this occurs is through wave motion. When a stone is dropped into a pond, at first only the moving stone has energy. But after a while, a leaf on the far side of the pond will bob up and down as the ripples reach it. Now the leaf has energy, too. The ripples have transported some of the stone's energy across the pond. Water waves or ripples are just one kind of wave. They are called transverse waves because, while the waves move outward from their source, the individual water particles move up and down only at right angles to the wave's direction. Another kind of wave is called the longitudinal wave. In these waves the particles move back and forth in the same direction as the wave. Sound waves are of this type.

ENERGY RAMPANT
The enormous energy of a huge ocean wave comes from the wind blowing across large stretches of sea. The surfer uses this energy to accelerate and drive the board.

A TRANSVERSE WAVE
Like a water wave, the wave traveling down a rope is a transverse wave. Each particle in turn is pulled up or down by the movement of its left-hand neighbor as the wave moves from left to right. In a longitudinal wave, particles knock each other along in the direction that the wave is traveling.

DEFINING A WAVE
The distance between successive wave ripples is called the wavelength. The number of waves passing any point each second is called the frequency. The size of the up-and-down movement is called the amplitude.

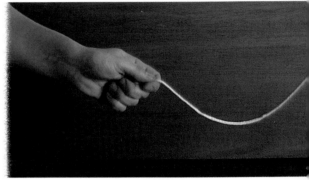

ADDING WAVES
This 18th-century apparatus shows the effect of combining two waves – an effect called "interference." A row of brass rods are cut to different lengths so that their tops form a wave shape. A wooden template in the form of another wave is slid underneath the rods. The tops of the rods now trace the combination of the two waves. Where the crests of the waves are above each other, the waves reinforce each other and the amplitude of the combined wave is greater than either of the two original waves. When the crest of one wave aligns with the trough of the other, the waves cancel each other out, producing a flat region where there is no wave activity.

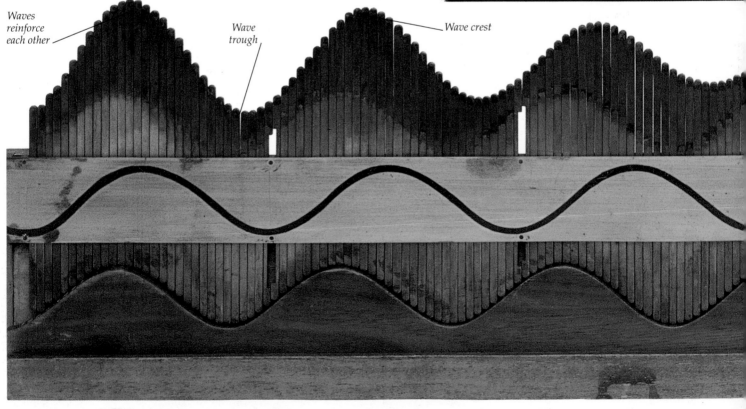

Waves reinforce each other

Wave trough

Wave crest

A GROWING BABY

An eight-week-old baby inside the womb is shown in orange and yellow in this image created by ultrasound – sound waves with frequencies so high that they cannot be heard by humans. Audible sounds have frequencies of between 20 and 20,000 vibrations per second, while ultrasounds have frequencies above 20,000 vibrations per second. The ultrasound waves are reflected at the boundaries between different kinds of tissue, such as muscle and bone. In an ultrasound scanner, a computer uses information about the reflected waves to create a picture of the growing baby.

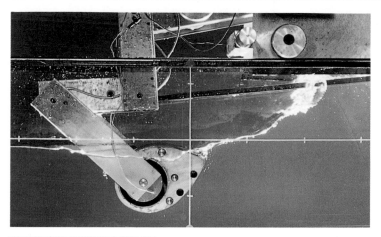

CLEAN ENERGY FROM THE SEA

The power of ocean waves offers a rich source of energy. This working model of "Salter's duck," being tested in a wave tank, absorbs a high proportion of each wave's energy and converts it into electricity. The up-and-down motion of the water, as a wave passes through from right to left, causes the oval-shaped "duck," designed by British scientist Professor Stephen Salter, to nod up and down. This turns a dynamo inside it and generates electricity.

SEEING WITH SOUND

Bats can "see" in the dark by using ultrasound. They emit short bursts, or clicks, of high-frequency sound waves. The waves bounce off trees and flying insects and produce an echo that the bat can hear. The shorter the time between a click and its echo, the closer the insect. As the bat approaches its target it emits more frequent clicks, allowing it to locate the insect with ever greater accuracy.

LIGHT PATTERNS

Light is made of ripples of electricity and magnetism called electromagnetic waves. This pattern of colored bands is caused by interference between light waves being reflected from the front of a film of soap and light waves being reflected back inside the film. This produces bands of light at different wavelengths and therefore of different colors.

Crest and trough "interfere" to produce no wave activity

Brass rods

Wooden template

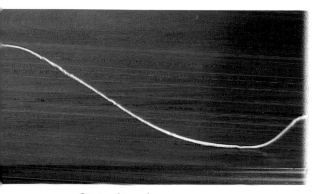

Around in circles

IF A BUCKET OF WATER IS SWUNG in a circle on the end of a rope, the water will not spill out if the bucket is moving fast enough. This is because the water is trying to continue in a straight line and therefore pushes against the bucket that is pulling it around in a circle. This tendency to continue moving in a straight line appears to produce a force acting away from the center. This illusory force is sometimes referred to as centrifugal force. The real force acting towards the center of the circle to keep the bucket moving in a circular path is called centripetal force. It is provided by the rope. Without this force, the bucket would fly off in a straight line. The faster the bucket is swung, the greater the centripetal force needed to prevent it from flying off.

Sack of seed

Handle to spin plate

Spinning plate

Arm to push the seed around

SEED SCATTERER
This late 19th-century seed scatterer shows centrifugal force at work. Seeds from the bag at the top fall on to a plate that is being turned by the handle. Arms on the spinning plate push the seeds round, but centrifugal force pushes the seeds away from the center to the edge of the plate where they fly off in straight lines. Centrifugal forces arise because moving objects always attempt to continue traveling in a straight line. This quality is called inertia (p. 30). Any object moving in a circle is continuously being forced to change direction. The inertia of the object resists this change and seems to produce a force that acts away from the center.

DAVID AND GOLIATH
This stone carving illustrates the Biblical Old Testament story in which David slays Goliath with a stone from his sling. The sling provides a centripetal force to restrain the stone while it is accelerated around. When one end of the sling is released, the moving stone flies off in a straight line, propelled by centrifugal force.

UP AND OVER

As a trick cyclist loops the loop, the pressure of the track against his tires provides the centripetal force to pull him around in a circle. As he goes over the top, gravity is pulling him down, but his tendency to travel on in a straight line (so-called centrifugal force) keeps the bicycle pressed outwards against the track. To complete a loop safely, the rider must be going fast, so he needs a long ramp down which to gain speed.

CENTRIFUGAL GOVERNOR

In the 18th century this device was used to control the gap between the millstones in a windmill. The turning sails drove a rope that spun the governor around. Centrifugal force caused the two weights to be thrown out, raising the boss at the bottom, which was attached to one of the millstones. Similar governors were used on steam engines to control the flow of steam and keep the engine speed constant.

Bowl for unseparated milk

Supply tap

Separator mechanism

Outlet for milk

Outlet for cream

Driving gear operated by handle on back

Rope driven pulley wheel

Heavy weight

Boss to raise millstone

THE CENTRIFUGE

This 1930s cream separator works by spinning the milk very rapidly. The heavier part of the milk is spun away from the center with a greater force than the cream, which is less dense, and the two parts can therefore be separated. A similar kind of centrifuge is used in laboratories to separate the heavier red cells from the lighter plasma in blood.

AROUND THE BEND

A racing motorcyclist leans into a tight corner to counteract the tendency of the bike to continue traveling forward in a straight line. The grip of the tires on the track provides a centripetal force toward the center of the turn. Steeply banked corners provide additional centripetal force and make turning at speed easier and safer.

FLOATING IN SPACE

An astronaut "walking" in space appears to have no forces acting on him. In fact he is continuously falling towards the earth under the influence of gravity. However, at the same time, his forward momentum produces a tendency to continue in a straight line, and the overall result is that he travels in a circular orbit around the earth. If his speed were to increase, he would fly off into space.

Spiraling in

SPINNING SKATER
An ice skater shows the conservation of angular momentum in action. The speed of rotation increases as the skater's arms are pulled in to the body.

A FAN OR CLOTHES DRYER continues to spin after its power is turned off. This is because, like all moving objects, a spinning object has momentum, but in this case it is momentum in a circle rather than straight-line momentum. A spinning object is said to have "angular momentum" and, like linear momentum (p. 30), this increases with speed and with mass. Surprisingly, angular momentum also depends upon the shape and size of the object. For example, if two wheels have the same mass but different diameters, the larger wheel will have the greater angular momentum when rotating. Like linear momentum, angular momentum is conserved; it does not change unless a force acts upon the object. One effect of the conservation of momentum is that changes in the shape of a spinning object will change its speed of rotation. It is for this reason that when the arms of a spinning ice skater are pulled in to the body, reducing the skater's diameter, the speed at which the skater spins increases. If the speed remained the same, angular momentum would have been lost rather than conserved.

Ball in position 2

DOWN THE PLUGHOLE
A whirlpool, or vortex, can occur spontaneously wherever a fluid (a gas or a liquid) flows through a hole. It is a very efficient form of flow. As the fluid spirals in to the center it speeds up, conserving its angular momentum. The whirlpool above occurs at a reservoir in France, but the same kind of vortex can be seen whenever water flows out of a bathtub or a sink. In theory, the earth's rotation should cause water to spiral in a counterclockwise direction in the northern hemisphere and in a clockwise direction in the southern hemisphere, but in practice the direction depends upon other factors, like the initial direction in which the water is moving.

WATERSPOUT
A waterspout occurs when a tornado (p. 55) passes over a body of water. The wind speeds up as it spirals in toward an area of low pressure at the center, and it acts like an inverted whirlpool, sucking water and spray up into the air. Water spouts are usually between 15 and 33 ft (5–10 m) across and can be up to 330 ft (100 m) high. The weather conditions that produce them are most common in tropical regions.

IN A WHIRL

Together, four superimposed images taken at equal time intervals reveal how a spiral motion speeds up. When the small ball, which is attached by a string to the central pole, is swung around, the string winds around the central rod and causes the ball to follow a spiral path. As the ball approaches the center the radius of its path decreases, and so the ball moves faster, since its angular momentum must be conserved. In the first time interval the ball has traveled from position 1 to position 2 – approximately one third of a circle. In the last time interval it has traveled from 3 to 4 – almost half a circle. Several different shapes of spiral are found in nature. This one is called Archimedes' Spiral, after its discoverer.

Ball in position 3

Spiral track

Ball in position 1

Ball in position 4

FUNNEL OF DESTRUCTION

A tornado, or twister, in which winds spiral into the center and speed up as they do so, is the most destructive type of storm known. The worst tornado on record occurred on March 18th, 1925. In three hours it tore a 220-mile (350-km) path through the states of Missouri, Illinois, and Indiana, killing 689 people, injuring almost 3,000 more, hurling cars into the air, and demolishing buildings.

THE RED SPOT

The spirals that are seen in weather systems are due to the fact that the earth is spinning. This causes winds to move in spirals rather than straight lines – the tornado is an extreme case of this. The famous Red Spot on Jupiter is a giant spiral storm that has been raging for more than 300 years. Winds spiral upward from the lower atmosphere and then spread out. The area of the storm is three times larger than the earth – about 24,000 miles (38,500 km) long by 7,000 miles (11,000 km) wide.

SPIRAL ELECTRON

A single electron moving through a magnetic field flies in a spiral path. As the electron loses energy, the magnetic field has a steadily greater influence on the electron, causing it to curl more and more tightly. The track is revealed in an apparatus called a bubble chamber, in which the particle leaves a trail of minute bubbles.

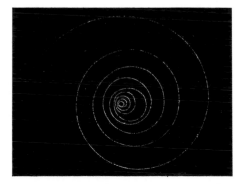

Spinning tops

A SPINNING TOP is a fascinating toy. It can be made to balance on the end of a pencil, and if the pencil is moved the spinning top remains pointing in the same direction. This happens because the top has angular momentum (p. 54), and this momentum does not change unless a force acts on the spinning top – angular momentum is always conserved. Spinning tops, or their more sophisticated cousins called gyroscopes, are used in compasses because they resist changes to the axis of their spin.
When a spinning top slows down, it leans to one side. Gravity is pulling the spinning top down, but it does not fall. Instead it slowly circles around its balance point. The spinning object converts the vertical force of gravity into a horizontal motion. This is known as precession.

THE GYROSCOPE
This 19th-century gyroscope is a piece of precision engineering. It consists of a wheel-shaped rotor on an axle that is mounted inside a metal ring. The rotor is set spinning by winding a string around the axle and then giving it a strong pull. This gyroscope has been suspended upright from a string attached to its base. One would expect it to simply fall and hang upside down, but in fact the spinning gyroscope precesses – it leans at an angle and swings around in a horizontal circle.

Rotor

Axle

Ring

JAPANESE TOPS
An old Japanese print shows children playing with spinning tops, seeing who can keep a top going the longest. A top is set spinning by pulling a string wrapped around its axle. Once it is spinning fast, a top is amazingly stable. Tops will right themselves if knocked and can even be made to balance on the edge of a knife.

MECHANICAL TIGHTROPE WALKER
Demonstrating the properties of the gyroscope, this 19th-century apparatus balances on a stretched string. The ring holding the spinning rotor is attached to a pole with a ball at each end, like that used by a circus high-wire walker. If the device tilts in one direction, the gyroscope swings the other way and the balancing pole corrects the tilt. The term "gyroscope" was first used by Léon Foucault (p. 47) in 1852.

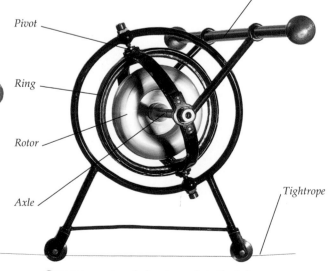

Balancing pole

Pivot

Ring

Rotor

Axle

Tightrope

Apparatus starts to tilt to the right

Gyroscope swings balancing pole to the left

DEFYING GRAVITY

The explanation of the gyroscope's strange behavior involves complicated mathematics and the use of Newton's Laws (p. 30). According to these laws, any force acting upon a spinning object will cause it to move at right angles to the force. The force of gravity acts downward and therefore causes the gyroscope to move around horizontally.

THE BICYCLE AS A GYROSCOPE

The spinning wheels of a bicycle act as gyros[copes], [keeping the] bike upright. Like all gyroscopes, the wheels [stay in] the same plane, giving the bicycle stability. A [bicycle is] steered by leaning to one side, without touching [the handlebars. The] sideways force produced by leaning is converted [into a force that makes] the wheels precess. This makes the bicycle easier [to steer.]

Tip of axis [over] which trav[els] as the globe [precess]es

Globe

THE EARTH AS A GYROSCOPE

The axis of the spinning earth is remarkably stable but our planet does precess very slightly, as shown by this 19th-century model. The earth takes 25,800 years for each circular wobble. This precession is largely caused by the gravitational pull of the sun and moon on the earth's equatorial bulge. It is thought that the tilting of the earth's axis in relation to the sun may be one of the causes of the Ice Ages.

Hollow conical base resting on pointed support

GYROSCOPES FOR STABILIZATION

The sights on the top of this early 20th-century ship's navigational sighting device are mounted on a frame that is stabilized by a gyroscope. Because of their ability to remain stable, gyroscopes have even been used to stabilize oceangoing ships. The Italian liner *Conte di Savois*, built in 1933, had three giant gyroscopes fitted as stabilizers. Each one was 13 ft (4 m) across and weighed more than 100 tons. Such large stabilizers were found to be too unwieldy, but smaller gyroscopes are still used to control the movements of stabilizing fins. These project from the hulls of ships to counteract the effects of the rolling seas.

Sights

Plate mounted on gyroscope frame

Gyroscope rotor

GYROSCOPES FOR GUIDANCE

This piece of equipment is a gyrocompass. It was used to guide a World War II V2 rocket during the powered section of its flight, after which the rocket went into ballistic flight (p. 27). Inside a gyrocompass, a spinning gyroscope maintains a constant orientation. The gyrocompass was invented by American engineer Elmer Sperry, and was first used in the US Navy ship *Delaware* in 1911.

Gyroscope

1985-417

Handle to spin rotor

Weight to hold gyroscope vertical

The ultimate speed limit

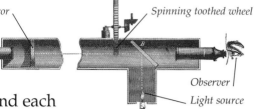

IN 1905 GERMAN SCIENTIST ALBERT EINSTEIN published a revolutionary new theory. It was called the Special Theory of Relativity and it dealt with the effects of high-speed motion. Einstein realized that when objects approach the speed of light – about 186,000 miles/second – common sense is an unreliable guide. If two cars are heading toward each other, and each is traveling at 100 mph, an observer in one of the cars would see the other car approaching at 200 mph. That is common sense. But if one of the cars is replaced by a beam of light, common sense would suggest that an observer in the car would see the light approaching at a speed that is 100 mph faster than 186,000 miles/second. Strangely, the light actually approaches at its usual speed. In fact, as Einstein realized, whatever speed an observer travels, the light always approaches at the same speed. How is this possible? After much thought, Einstein showed that for the speed of light to be always the same, distances must shrink and time must slow down at near-light speeds. Einstein also showed that matter can be transformed into energy and that the mass of an object increases with speed. This makes it increasingly difficult to accelerate objects as they approach near-light speeds. In fact, nothing can travel faster than the speed of light and only electromagnetic waves, such as light, can travel that fast. It is the ultimate speed limit.

Mirror — **Spinning toothed wheel** — **Observer** — **Light source**

THE SPEED OF LIGHT

The speed of light is 186,000 miles (300,000 kilometers) per second – 10,000 times faster than the fastest rocket. At this speed, a rocket could travel around the world seven times in one second. The first reliable measurement of the speed of light was made by French scientist Armand Fizeau (1819-1896) in 1849. He directed light at a distant mirror and measured its time of travel by spinning a toothed wheel in the path of the beam. The beam departed through a gap in the toothed wheel and was blocked by the following tooth. Knowing the speed of revolution of the wheel, Fizeau could calculate the time of travel of the beam and hence its speed.

Albert Michelson (1852-1931)

Edward Morley (1838-1923)

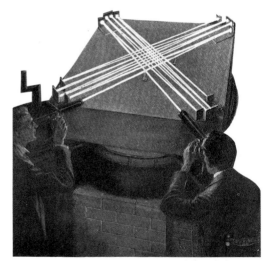

MICHELSON-MORLEY EXPERIMENT

In 1887 American physicists Albert Michelson and Edward Morley carried out an experiment. A beam of light was split into two parts moving at right angles to each other and then brought together again. The experiment produced an unexpected result: the speed of light was the same whether the beam was traveling in the same direction as the earth's motion or at right angles to it. Michelson and Morley had found that the speed of the earth's motion did not affect the speed of the light beam. This fact is central to the theory of relativity: the speed of light remains the same for all observers, no matter how fast they are moving.

IT IS TIME ITSELF THAT CHANGES

Two rockets are traveling past the earth, at a fixed distance apart, at almost the speed of light. A flash of light is sent from one ship to the other. To the astronauts aboard the rockets, the light is seen to travel in a straight line between them. However, since the rockets are moving forward at high speed, to an observer on the earth the light beam appears to follow a diagonal path. This diagonal path is clearly longer than the direct distance between the rockets. Since the speed of light is constant, the passage of the light beam between the rockets must therefore seem to take longer when seen from earth. Although the observers on the rockets and on the earth have witnessed the same event, they make different judgements about the time taken. In other words, time does not pass at the same rate for all observers. If the rockets were passing the earth at 90 percent of the speed of light, the earth-bound observer would see the beam take 2.3 times longer to cross than would the crew of the rocket. This also means that the observer on the earth is aging 2.3 times as fast as the astronauts.

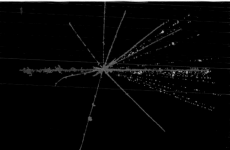

ALBERT EINSTEIN
As a young man, Albert Einstein (1879-1955) was thought to be rather dull. One of his school reports read, "He will never amount to anything." Yet he proved to be a scientific genius. Einstein's ideas about forces and motion were so revolutionary that many people, including members of the scientific community, could not believe them. In 1905 he published his Special Theory of Relativity, describing how objects behave when traveling at near-light speed. In 1916 he published the General Theory of Relativity, which extended his ideas. He received the Nobel Prize for Physics in 1921. He emigrated to the USA in 1933 to avoid persecution by the Nazis.

PROVING EINSTEIN RIGHT
Many experiments have proved Einstein's amazing ideas to be correct. In 1971 very sensitive "atomic" clocks were carried around the world in high-speed aircraft and then compared with clocks left on the ground. The clocks that had traveled at high speed were found to have slowed down by 0.0000001 seconds – enough to prove Einstein correct. Cosmic rays provide another proof. These high-speed particles reach the earth's atmosphere from space and normally exist for only a brief time. But because they are traveling at such high speeds, time slows down for them and some can survive for long enough to be detected within the Earth's atmosphere.

Einstein's gravity

ARTHUR EDDINGTON (1882-1944)
The English astronomer and mathematician Arthur Eddington led the expedition to Príncipe, in the Atlantic, that confirmed Einstein's radical new ideas about gravity.

"LIGHT CAUGHT BENDING" screamed a newspaper headline in 1919. The event being reported was an expedition led by English astronomer Arthur Eddington to the island of Príncipe, off the west coast of Africa. The purpose of the expedition was to measure the position of stars during an eclipse of the sun. Albert Einstein had predicted that light from the stars would be affected by the sun's gravity. According to Einstein, space acts as if it were a stretched rubber sheet. When a heavy object is placed on the sheet it creates a dip or hollow. A small ball rolled across the sheet will be affected by the dip and will roll towards the heavy object. This is the way that gravity acts, according to Einstein. If a light beam travels across the sheet, it too will follow the curves of the sheet, and the beam will be bent. Eddington had observed the stars' light rays being bent by the sun's gravity, and overnight Einstein became famous. His theory of gravity, which he called the General Theory of Relativity, became the talk of the scientific community. Einstein's theory was even able to explain the fact that Mercury's orbit around the sun twists a little each year. Newton's theory of gravity could not explain why this happens, but Einstein's theory could. This convinced most scientists that Einstein's view of gravity was correct.

EINSTEIN'S CROSS
This image shows the effect of gravity on light. The central spot is a relatively close quasar, or starlike object. The four surrounding spots are images of a distant quasar behind the near one. The nearby quasar acts like a giant lens, bending the light from the far one and producing four images. Einstein predicted this gravitational lens effect in 1936.

The rubber sheet of space-time is distorted by the presence of a massive object

Path of passing comet

Sun

RUBBER-SHEET GRAVITY
Of course Einstein did not suggest that there really was a rubber sheet stretched through space. However, his work showed that there was something called "space-time" which acted like a rubber sheet. Space-time is difficult to visualize: it is a combination of space and time. Einstein had to use complicated mathematics to explain the properties of space-time. This model shows an object, perhaps a comet, passing the sun in a curved path. Newton would have explained the curved path by saying that there is a force – gravity – which is attracting the object to the sun. Einstein, on the other hand, said that the object's path is curved because the sun distorts space and time around it.

THE BLACK HOLE

A black hole is like a very small, very heavy ball on the "rubber sheet" of space-time, creating a deep narrow dent into which nearby objects fall. The gravity is so strong that once something has been attracted toward the black hole, it can never escape from it. Not even light can escape from black holes – that is why they appear black. This picture is an artist's impression of a black hole with a giant blue star in the background. A stream of gas is being pulled from the atmosphere of the blue star by the immense gravity of the black hole. As the gas spirals into the black hole, it forms a flat disc that heats up and emits X-rays, creating the central white region.

BLACK HOLE EXPLORER

English physicist Stephen Hawking is Professor of Mathematics at Cambridge University, the post once held by Isaac Newton. Confined to a wheelchair for many years because of a muscular disease, Hawking has worked to combine Einstein's theory of gravity with quantum physics, which explains the structure of atoms. Quantum theory describes how random chance plays a part in the events of the subatomic world, an idea that Einstein was never able to accept. Disputing the role of chance, Einstein once said, "I shall never believe that God plays dice with the world." To this Hawking replies that "God not only plays dice, he throws them where they can't be seen." Hawking has discovered that the strong gravity around a black hole can produce particles of matter. He has also used Einstein's theories to explore the very early history of the universe.

SPACEWARPS

Gravitational waves are ripples in space-time, similar to ripples traveling across a rubber sheet. Einstein's theory suggests that cataclysmic events in space, such as the explosions of stars, might produce these waves. Gravitational wave detectors, like the one here, consist of large blocks of metal. The experimenters use lasers to look for inexplicable shudders in the metal, caused by one of these waves. So far, no such waves have been detected, despite a 20-year search.

Comet's path is bent into a curve by the distortion of space and time produced by the sun's mass

The fundamental forces

THE MAGNETIC FORCE
Magnetism, which has a strong effect on metals like iron and steel but less effect on other materials, arises because of tiny electric currents within the atoms of the magnet.

THE FASTEST OBJECTS ON EARTH are the tiny particles used in experiments to investigate sub-atomic particles and forces. Inside giant machines called accelerators, these particles reach speeds approaching the speed of light, and then smash together with far greater energy than any natural collision on earth. The collision creates a shower of new particles which explode in a starburst of fragments. Inside an accelerator the particles reach speeds of more than 99.99 percent of the speed of light. At these speeds, the effects predicted by Einstein's Special Theory of Relativity (p. 58) can be observed. Careful measurements show that particles called muons, which normally only live for about two millionths of a second, have their lifetimes extended by 20 times inside an accelerator, as predicted by Einstein's theory. The mass of the moving particles is also seen to increase as the speed rises. Einstein said that matter and energy are interchangeable, and new particles are indeed created from the energy of the speeding particles. Scientists can identify these particles and study the forces acting on them. Forces unknown in everyday life are found at work between the particles that make up the atomic nucleus. These are the strong nuclear force and the weak nuclear force. It is now possible to see that there are just a few basic forces acting in the universe – electromagnetic forces, gravitational forces, and the strong and weak nuclear forces. All other forces are derived from these fundamental forces.

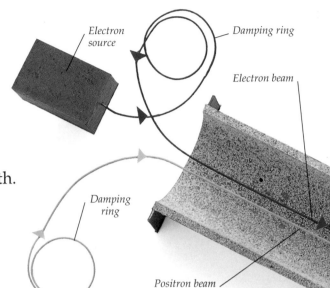

Electron source

Damping ring

Electron beam

Damping ring

Positron beam

INSIDE AN ACCELERATOR
In this schematic model of the Stanford Linear Accelerator, electrons (red) and positively charged electrons, called positrons (yellow), are accelerated along the straight 2-mile (3-km) tube and then steered into a head-on collision. An electron source fires bunches of electrons down the track via the damping ring. The damping ring squeezes the electron bursts into short pulses. About halfway along the track, some electrons are diverted to a target, where they create positrons. These positrons are injected into the head of the accelerator tube and are fired down the tube with the electrons. Magnets guide the beams to the final collision, which is studied inside the massive 1,600-ton particle detector.

THE ELECTROMAGNETIC FORCE
The electromagnetic force is one of the fundamental forces and is responsible for binding atoms together to form molecules. Every aspect of life depends on this force. Electromagnetic forces hold the molecules of the body together and maintain the structure of all physical objects. The chemical reactions that release energy from food and make it possible for muscles to do work are rearrangements of electrical charges in atoms and molecules, as is the process of burning. Electromagnetic forces are driving this train along its single track.

ELECTROMAGNETISM
This electric motor was made in 1840 by the English physicist Charles Wheatstone (1802-1875). It demonstrates that a flowing electric current produces a magnetic field. Equally, a magnet can produce electricity in a wire. Electricity and magnetism are two different aspects of a single force called electromagnetism.

Iron rotor

Electricity flows through coil of wire around iron bar, creating magnetic field

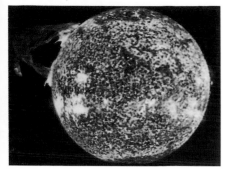

THE STRENGTH OF THE FORCES
The energy that powers the sun comes from the fusion of atomic nuclei. The sun would cease to shine without the forces that hold nuclei together. The strong nuclear force is the strongest of all the forces – 100 times as strong as the electromagnetic force. However, the strong force has a very short range. Its influence is only ever felt within the atomic nucleus. The weak force, too, is felt only within the nucleus. It is 100,000 million times weaker than the electromagnetic force. The force of gravity is the weakest of all; it is around a million million million million million million times weaker than the weak nuclear force. However, it is a long range force (p. 32) and can be felt across the universe.

ABDUS SALAM
Pakistani physicist Abdus Salam is known for his work on the fundamental forces. In 1979 he was the first from his country to receive a Nobel Prize. With Americans Sheldon Glashow and Steven Weinberg he proved that the electromagnetic force and the weak nuclear force were variations of a single underlying "superforce," called the electroweak force. His ideas were verified experimentally in 1973 at CERN (*Conseil Européen pour la Recherche Nucléaire*), in Geneva, Switzerland. Scientists are now investigating the possibility that all the fundamental forces are variations of a single force.

Positron source

Arc-bending magnets

Focusing magnets

Focusing magnets

Arc-bending magnets

Particle collision detector

THE STRAIGHTEST LINE
At the Stanford Linear Accelerator, in California, electromagnetic forces are used to speed particles along a track. The track is so straight that its supports have to be of different heights to allow for the curvature of the Earth. The straight-line arrangement at Stanford is unusual; most large accelerators are circular. The Stanford accelerator was used to discover the psi particle and to measure the lifetime of a particle called the Z^0 (Z zero), which helps carry the weak nuclear force.

PARTICLE COLLISION
This is an artifically colored photograph showing the tracks of subatomic particles colliding. It was produced at CERN, the European particle physics laboratory. The complex tangle of tracks can be analyzed by computers to reveal the forces at work. Modern theories suggest that all the fundamental forces are "carried" by particles that flit between other particles. The strong nuclear force is carried by particles called "gluons," the weak force by the Z and W particles, electromagnetism by the photon, and gravity by a particle called the graviton.

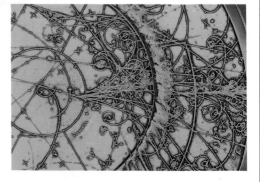

Index

Acknowledgments

Dorling Kindersley would like to thank: John Becklake, Neil Brown, Anna Bunney, Helen Dowling, Stewart Emmens, Sam Evans, Peter Fitzgerald, Graeme Fyffe, Ben Gammon, Alex Hayward, Jane Insley, Kevin Johnson, John Liffen, Barry Marshall & the staff of the Science Museum Workshop, Robert McWilliam, Douglas Millard, Alan Morton, Andrew Nahum, Cathy Needham, Keith Packer, David Ray and his staff, Fiona Reid, Francesca Riccini, John Robinson, Ken Shirt, Jane Smith, Victoria Smith, John Smith, Peter Stephens, Peter Tomlinson, Denys Vaughan, Tony Vincent, Jane Wess, David Woodcock and Michael Wright for advice and help with the provision of objects for photography; Reg Grant and Jack Challoner for help in the initial stages of the book; David Donkin and Peter Griffiths for the model making; Deborah Rhodes for page makeup; Karl Adamson for assistance with the photography; Susannah Steel and Stephanie Jackson for proofreading.

Picture research Deborah Pownall and Catherine O'Rourke
Illustrations Janos Marffy and John Woodcock
Index Jane Parker

Picture credits

t=top b=bottom c=center l=left r=right

Allsport /Richard Martin 57tl; /Mike Powell 31tc; /Pascall Rondeau 53cr. Ancient Art and Architecture 7cr. Arcaid /Barbara Godzikowska 43tl. Ardea /Peter Steyn 17c; /Francois Gohier 39br. Bridgeman Art Library 25tr. British Library 17bl. British Museum 11c. Brown Brothers 58cr; 58br. Bruce Coleman /Goetz D. Plage 44tl. Camera Press 61cr. Colorsport /Dickinson 30tr. Culver Pictures 58bl. ET Archive 56cl. Mary Evans Picture Library 7c; 7br; 12tl; 17tc; 17tr; 17cr; 18bl; 19br; 24cl; 43c; 44bc; 46bc; 48tl; 53tl; 54bc. Glasgow University, Department of Physics and Astronomy 61cl. Haags Gementemuseum 47tl. Sonia Halliday Photographs 52br. Robert Harding Picture Library 6cr; 15cr; 43cr; /Philip Craven 33br. Michael Holford 7tr. Hulton Picture Co. 39tr; 40tl; 63tr; /Bettman Archives 59br. Image Bank 31tr; /Patrick Doherty 37tl; /Guido Rossi 41tl; /Terry Williams 41br. Kings College, Cambridge 29tr. Kobal 19bc; 22tl. Frank Lane Picture Library 31c; /David Hoadley 55tr. Mansell Collection 36tl; 43tr. Memtek International 49c. NASA 55cr. National Portrait Gallery, London 21tr; 28cl. Peter Newark's Military Pictures 37bl. Pictor 54tl. Pierpont Morgan Library, New York 10tr. Popperfoto 27tr. Réunion des Musées Nationaux cover front cr. Ann Ronan Picture Library 10tl; 10cl; 11tr; 15cl; 16c; 23tl; 25br; 26tl; 26bl; 26br; 27tl; 32tr; 33tr; 34c; 38br; 44cl; 47cl; 58tr. Prof. Stephen Salter 51tr. Scala 24bl. Science Museum Photo Library, London 12cr; 15tc; 20br; 44cr; 47tc; 47cr; 60tl. Science Photo Library 29cr; /Alex Bartel 41tc; 62bl; /Lawrence Berkley 37br; 55br; /Julian Baum 61tc; /Dr Jeremy Burgess 33tl; /J.L. Charmet 32cl; /CNRI 51tr /Prof. Harold Edgerton 37tr; /Malcolm Fielding, Johnson Matthey PLC 49tr; /Clive Freeman, The Royal Institution 43br; /Patrick Loiez, Cern 63br; /NASA 31tr; 63tl; /P. Powell, C. Powell & D. Perkins 59cr; /John Sanford 37tc; /David Scharf 39cl; /Francoise Sauze 54cl; /Space Telescope Science Institute & NASA 60cl; /Stanford Linear Accelerator Centre 63bl. Ian Whitelaw 6bl. Wurttembergische Landesbibliotehek Stuttgart 19tr. Zefa cover front c; 6cl; 8tl; 13tl; 30tl; 42tl; 49cr; /Don James 50tr; /K. Jung 49tl; /J. W. Myers 6br; /Madison 38tl; /T. Sanders 42bl; /Steeger 50cl; /E.H. White 53br.

With the exception of the items listed above, and the objects on pages 2tl, 2bl, 6-7, 8-9b, 9cl, 9tr, 10b, 12-13b, 14l, 14-15c, 15r, 15br, 17lc, 23c, 25bc, 30-31b, 36-37, 39, 42-43, 45b, 48-49, 52l, 54-55, 60-61, 62-63c, all the photographs in this book are of objects in the collections of the Science Museum, London.

1 BIRD	**2** ROCKS & MINERALS	**3** SKELETON	**4** ARMS & ARMOR	**5** TREE	**6** POND & RIVER	**7** BUTTERFLY & MOTH	**8** SPORTS
9 SHELL	**10** EARLY HUMANS	**11** MAMMAL	**12** MUSIC	**13** DINOSAUR	**14** PLANT	**15** SEASHORE	**16** FLAG
17 INSECT	**18** MONEY	**19** FOSSIL	**20** FISH	**21** CAR	**22** FLYING MACHINE	**23** ANCIENT EGYPT	**24** ANCIENT ROME
25 CRYSTAL & GEM	**26** REPTILE	**27** INVENTION	**28** WEATHER	**29** CAT	**30** BIBLE LANDS	**31** EXPLORER	**32** DOG
33 HORSE	**34** FILM	**35** COSTUME	**36** BOAT	**37** ANCIENT GREECE	**38** VOLCANO & EARTHQUAKE	**39** TRAIN	**40** SHARK
41 AMPHIBIAN	**42** ELEPHANT	**43** KNIGHT	**44** MUMMY	**45** COWBOY	**46** WHALE	**47** AZTEC, INCA & MAYA	**48** BOOK
49 CASTLE	**50** VIKING	**51** DESERT	**52** PREHISTORIC LIFE	**53** PYRAMID	**54** JUNGLE	**55** ANCIENT CHINA	**56** ARCHEOLOGY
57 ARCTIC & ANTARCTIC	**58** BUILDING	**59** PIRATE	**60** NORTH AMERICAN INDIAN	**61** AFRICA	**62** OCEAN	**63** BATTLE	**64** GORILLA, MONKEY & APE
65 MEDIEVAL LIFE	**66** FARM	**67** SPY	**68** RELIGION	**69** EAGLE & BIRDS OF PREY	**70** WITCHES & MAGIC-MAKERS	**71** SPACE EXPLORATION	**72** SHIPWRECK